T0295546

Customer Data Sharing Frameworks

The proliferation of open banking and open finance regimes across the globe demonstrates an ever-increasing interest of policymakers in empowering customers to take control of their data through innovative data sharing frameworks. These frameworks mostly operate within a single (e.g., financial services) sector but are poised to extend to other parts of the economy in the future – and eventually apply economy-wide.

This book articulates the concept of economy-wide customer data sharing (CDS) frameworks, analyses in detail the main challenges associated with the development of such frameworks and is informed by the lessons learned from Australia's world-first, cross-sectoral Consumer Data Right regime. It develops a first comprehensive taxonomy of CDS frameworks and offers valuable insights on crucial issues of customer trust, information security, consumer protection and participant regulation.

This study, apart from its scholarly importance, has clear practical value. It formulates 12 lessons that will assist governmental officials and other policymakers engaged in establishing and revising data sharing frameworks across the globe. It is essential reading for anyone interested or involved in the law and policy related to the sharing of a most precious resource in the modern economy – customer data.

Anton Didenko is a senior lecturer at the Faculty of Law and Justice, University of New South Wales (UNSW), Sydney, Australia.

Natalia Jevglevskaja is a research fellow at the Faculty of Law and Justice, University of New South Wales (UNSW), Sydney, Australia.

Ross P. Buckley is an Australian Research Council Laureate Fellow and a Scientia Professor at the University of New South Wales (UNSW), Sydney, Australia.

Routledge Focus on Economics and Finance

The fields of economics are constantly expanding and evolving. This growth presents challenges for readers trying to keep up with the latest important insights. Routledge Focus on Economics and Finance presents short books on the latest big topics, linking in with the most cutting-edge economics research.

Individually, each title in the series provides coverage of a key academic topic, whilst collectively the series forms a comprehensive collection across the whole spectrum of economics.

For more information about this series, please visit: www.routledge.com/ Routledge-Focus-on-Economics-and-Finance/book-series/RFEF

Customer Data Sharing Frameworks

Twelve Lessons for the World

Anton Didenko,
Natalia Jevglevskaja
and Ross P. Buckley

LONDON AND NEW YORK

First published 2024
by Routledge
4 Park Square, Milton Park, Abingdon, Oxon OX14 4RN

and by Routledge
605 Third Avenue, New York, NY 10158

Routledge is an imprint of the Taylor & Francis Group, an informa business

© 2024 Anton Didenko, Natalia Jevglevskaja and Ross P Buckley

The right of Anton Didenko, Natalia Jevglevskaja and Ross P Buckley to be identified as authors of this work has been asserted in accordance with Sections 77 and 78 of the Copyright, Designs and Patents Act 1988.

All rights reserved. No part of this book may be reprinted or reproduced or utilised in any form or by any electronic, mechanical, or other means, now known or hereafter invented, including photocopying and recording, or in any information storage or retrieval system, without permission in writing from the publishers.

Trademark notice: Product or corporate names may be trademarks or registered trademarks, and are used only for identification and explanation without intent to infringe.

British Library Cataloguing-in-Publication Data
A catalogue record for this book is available from the British Library

Library of Congress Cataloging-in-Publication Data
Names: Didenko, Anton, 1985- author. | Jevglevskaja, Natalia, author. | Buckley, Ross P., author.
Title: Customer data sharing frameworks : twelve lessons for the world / Anton Didenko, Natalia Jevglevskaja and Ross P. Buckley.
Description: Abingdon, Oxon ; New York, NY : Routledge, 2024. | Series: Routledge focus on economics and finance | Includes bibliographical references and index.
Identifiers: LCCN 2023052460 (print) | LCCN 2023052461 (ebook) | ISBN 9781032538983 (hardback) | ISBN 9781032538990 (paperback) | ISBN 9781003414216 (ebook)
Subjects: LCSH: Consumer profiling. | Consumer profiling—Data processing. | Data protection.
Classification: LCC HF5415.32 .D526 2024 (print) | LCC HF5415.32 (ebook) | DDC 658.3/34--dc23/eng/20231130
LC record available at https://lccn.loc.gov/2023052460
LC ebook record available at https://lccn.loc.gov/2023052461

ISBN: 978-1-032-53898-3 (hbk)
ISBN: 978-1-032-53899-0 (pbk)
ISBN: 978-1-003-41421-6 (ebk)

DOI: 10.4324/9781003414216

Typeset in Times New Roman
by Apex CoVantage,LLC

Contents

Foreword

Data is fundamental to customers and businesses. The information and knowledge which it can establish enables choices to be made and transactions to take place. In a digital economy, customer data is valuable and its sharing and use essential. However, the sharing of customer data can also produce harm when the data is misused. This balance of risk and reward makes the design of customer data sharing frameworks critical, so that they enable customers to share their data with those that they choose with the confidence that it will only be used as they ask.

The rapid development of these frameworks globally is why *Customer Data Sharing Frameworks* is such an important book. Through clear and accessible analysis, Anton, Natalia and Ross articulate the concept of economy-wide customer data sharing frameworks, set out the foundations on which these frameworks are established and recommend critical features for their future development. The distinguished authors' extensive research, experience and expertise are manifest in the book's insights on crucial issues of customer trust, information security, consumer protection and participant regulation.

This book is essential reading for those interested or involved in the law and policy related to the sharing of the valuable resource of customer data. It is a vital tool for those seeking to understand how the safe and effective sharing of data can be enabled, whether lawmakers or lawyers, data holders or data recipients, businesses or customers.

Dr Scott Farrell

Acknowledgements

We would like to thank the Australian government for funding this research through the Australian Research Council (Laureate project FL200100007 'The Financial Data Revolution: Seizing the Benefits, Controlling the Risks'). We wish to thank Scott Farrell and other colleagues at the Faculty of Law and Justice, University of New South Wales, for their invaluable insights; Andrew Lynch and Michael Handler, our Dean and Head of School, for their unstinting support; and Anna Ho, Jarrod Li and Nazim Rahman for invaluable research assistance.

We are grateful to the anonymous reviewers and the Routledge team, in particular Kristina Abbotts, who supported us greatly during the publication process.

Our concluding words of gratitude are for the people who are closest: our families. Thank you for helping us when it mattered most and for your endless love, patience and understanding. We needed your support as each of us have faced quite exceptional personal challenges during the writing of this book, and we have received this support in abundance, so our gratitude is immense.

Abbreviations

ABN	Australian Business Number
ACCC	Australian Competition and Consumer Commission
ADR	Accredited Data Recipient
AEMO	Australian Energy Market Operator
API	Application Programming Interface
APP	Australian Privacy Principle(s)
ASIC	Australian Securities and Investments Commission
CCA	Competition and Consumer Act 2010 (Cth) (Australia)
CDR	Consumer Data Right
CDS	Customer Data Sharing
CMA	Competition and Markets Authority (United Kingdom)
CSIRO	Commonwealth Scientific and Industrial Research Organisation (Australia)
DSB	Data Standards Body (Australia)
FCA	Financial Conduct Authority (United Kingdom)
GDPR	General Data Protection Regulation (European Union)
ISO	International Organization for Standardization
OAIC	Office of the Australian Information Commissioner
OBIE	Open Banking Implementation Entity (United Kingdom)
P2P	Peer-To-Peer
PFM	Personal Finance Management
PSD2	Revised Payment Services Directive (European Union)
SS	Screen-Scraping
UK	United Kingdom
US	United States

Chapter 1

Introduction

Abstract

This chapter briefly explains the reasons behind the emergence and ongoing evolution of *customer data sharing* (*CDS*) frameworks, which seek to upend the tradition of businesses tightly holding isolated 'silos' of valuable customer data. It identifies three generations of *CDS* frameworks, from rudimentary *CDS 1.0* regimes encompassing 'traditional' privacy and competition laws to sector-specific *CDS 2.0* rules (such as open banking and open finance), to *CDS 3.0* comprising bespoke laws to facilitate customer data sharing across multiple sectors and even across an entire economy. This chapter outlines the distinguishing features of third-generation customer data sharing frameworks, their key objectives and underlying data sharing mechanisms. Our focus is Australia's Consumer Data Right regime as the world's first implementation of *CDS 3.0.*

1.1 Customer data as a precious resource

Data drives today's digital economy. Online commerce platforms depend upon it. Artificial intelligence (AI) thrives or flounders on the quality of it. Finance has long depended upon it: 'the party that can obtain and control the flow of information ultimately gets the gold.'[1] This rule, first inspired by the major banking dynasties of the Renaissance and Industrial Revolution, is today more relevant than ever before. In the modern digital economy, information is truly 'the most precious commodity.'[2]

Different kinds of data underpin the modern economy. Among them, *customer data* – information held by businesses about customers, such as their financial position, transactions and preferences – is particularly significant. Access to customer data empowers businesses to offer more relevant and competitively priced services to current and prospective customers. It enables more efficient allocation of business resources and can generate substantial economic value, particularly when coupled with sophisticated forms of data analytics. In other words, customer data is valuable information and as such has a lot in common with customer money held digitally in a bank account, which also exists as data.[3]

DOI: 10.4324/9781003414216-1

Unlike money, however, customer data can be transferred to another and retained; it can be shared among many without losing value. It is, in technical terms, 'non-rivalrous.' It can be reused multiple times by applying different data processing algorithms without any loss of utility – generating new insights and value from the same data. Machine learning and other subsets of AI further boost the quality and accuracy of algorithms and enable businesses to extract ever more value from customer data, which further increases the demand for it.

However, customer data has historically remained 'siloed' within the organisations which have the technological and financial resources to collect and analyse it at scale, as well as strong incentives (both *legal* and *economic*) not to share the data with third parties. Such businesses must comply with many legal obligations – including duties to preserve bank secrecy/confidentiality[4] of customer banking data, to ensure privacy of personal information[5] and to observe information (or 'cyber') security regulations.[6] Furthermore, it is rational for data holders not to share customer data with their competitors: data being unavailable to new market entrants allows incumbent businesses to capitalise on information asymmetries.

National legal systems have begun to evolve to facilitate the sharing of customer data and upend the tradition of businesses holding customer data tightly and treating it as their own. In the absence of generally accepted terminology, in this book we call the resulting legal regimes *customer data sharing* (*CDS*) frameworks.

CDS frameworks are to today's economy what sanitation systems have been for centuries for cities. City living requires clear water to be piped in and sewage piped out, efficiently and safely. *CDS* regimes seek to do for the digital economy what sanitation systems do for our cities – make them habitable and fit for purpose. And just as water supply and sewage disposal need to be well designed and regulated to protect public health, customer data sharing needs to be well designed and regulated to protect the different stakeholders, especially consumers.

The evolution of *CDS* frameworks has accelerated in recent years, giving rise to innovative customer-focused legal reforms which have the potential to alter dramatically the way businesses treat customer data. We are now on the brink of a paradigm shift, a new way of thinking about customer data embedded in the law. To better understand the scope, magnitude and direction of change, in Sections 1.2–1.4, we distinguish *three generations* of *CDS* frameworks.

1.2 CDS 1.0: utilising pre-existing laws

The earliest attempts to facilitate the sharing of customer data – *CDS 1.0* – are characterised by the absence of bespoke *CDS* laws. In their first iteration, *CDS* frameworks view wider circulation of customer data as a welcome (side-)effect of pre-existing legal rules, rather than a primary objective. In other words, *CDS 1.0* may recognise the usefulness of sharing customer data but does not actively target the 'silos' of customer data held by incumbent organisations. At the time of writing, most *CDS* frameworks still fall into this category.

In practical terms, first-generation *CDS* frameworks tend to rely on privacy laws to enable the sharing of personal information, as well as competition laws to deal with the risks of data concentration and monopolisation. Unfortunately, the application of these laws to the sharing of customer data leaves substantial gaps in regulation, which generates inefficiency and leaves many customers, whose data is being shared, unprotected. As an example, the limited reach of privacy laws, which apply to personal information about individuals, makes them redundant for the purposes of sharing other types of data, such as data about legal entities. Furthermore, some recipients of customer data (such as small businesses)[7] may be exempted from the application of privacy laws, which generates strong incentives for customers to share their data only with large incumbent institutions. The application of 'general' competition laws is equally problematic, considering that these laws have largely failed to prevent the concentration of massive amounts of customer data within large institutions or address the resulting risks to competition.

First-generation *CDS* regimes rely heavily on customer consent to balance the interests of different stakeholders involved in the sharing of customer data. However, despite permitting the sharing of customer data in principle, *CDS 1.0* frameworks do little else to make such sharing safer, more convenient or economical. Customers are expected to do their own due diligence, find the right recipients and select appropriate channels to share their data. The ever-increasing volume of customer data and uses of such data make *CDS 1.0* regimes unfit for purpose. The inefficiencies mentioned in the previous paragraph force customers to seek alternative methods to share their data with new market entrants, such as screen-scraping (SS), which generate substantial security risks.[8]

These inherent limitations of *CDS 1.0* have prompted further legal reforms which culminated in the establishment of second-generation (*CDS 2.0*) sectoral *CDS* frameworks – built specifically to facilitate wider sharing of customer data. These are discussed next.

1.3   CDS 2.0: bespoke sectoral data sharing frameworks

Second-generation *CDS* frameworks are purpose-built to facilitate the sharing of customer data but are not expansive enough to apply across multiple sectors, let alone economy-wide. The nature and scope of *CDS 2.0* are perhaps best illustrated by the twin concepts of 'open banking' and 'open finance.'

The concept of 'open banking' captures various regulatory and industry-driven initiatives to induce commercial banks to share their customers' data with third parties so as to enable such parties to offer new or improved services. It has gained prominence in recent years, particularly following the introduction of a mandated data sharing framework for retail banks in the United Kingdom (UK) in 2017.[9] While there is no universally accepted definition of open banking, its key features were aptly summarised by Scott Farrell, who defines it as 'sharing customer banking data as the customer directs, for use as the customer desires.'[10] This simple definition helpfully emphasises the role of the customer as the source of shared data and controller of the data sharing process.

'Open finance' is a more recent concept that encapsulates the next step in the evolution of open banking – one that results in the wider sharing of customer data across the entire financial services sector. Compared to 'open banking,' 'open finance' is a broader category that covers customer data generated by *all* financial institutions, not just banks – although its exact boundaries are yet to be defined precisely.[11]

As an expansion of open banking, open finance seeks to level the informational playing field by breaking the customer data 'silos' across the entire financial services sector in an attempt to bring about market disruption in areas like online lending, payments, stock trading and investment.[12] However, the applications of shared data, while important in practice, are not the defining characteristic of open finance: after all, open banking data can be used to offer non-banking products as well. Instead, the principal difference between open banking and open finance lies in the *types of data* shared (banking or non-banking) and, consequently, the *types of businesses* that share such data (banks or other financial institutions). As a result, 'open finance' can be defined similarly to 'open banking' above as 'sharing customer *financial data* as the customer directs for use as the customer desires.'

In contrast to the approach taken by other authors,[13] neither of the two definitions above includes references to a particular technology (such as application programming interfaces or 'APIs'). This is intentional. A technology-neutral definition permits us to focus on the defining features of 'open banking' and 'open finance' (like types of data shared and customer control), rather than incidental elements (like enabling software protocols or data transmission channels) that are likely to change over time and across jurisdictions.

Nonetheless, it is worth noting the two main functional underpinnings of *CDS 2.0* at the time of writing: (i) data portability and (ii) data interoperability.

Data portability is defined by the International Organization for Standardization (ISO) as the 'ability to easily transfer data from one system to another without being required to re-enter data.'[14] It enables customers to obtain from one service provider a copy of their data that can be stored on the customer's own device in a form that can be sent to another service provider.[15] In such 'one-off' exports, the data platforms operated by the two service providers do not have to be connected, and the customer effectively acts as the intermediary which handles the data transfer.[16] As a result, the process of transferring data can be slow and may take hours on some platforms to complete.[17]

Data interoperability is defined by the ISO as the 'ability of two or more systems or applications to exchange information and to mutually use the information that has been exchanged.'[18] This important function makes requesting customer data and subsequently exchanging it across different software platforms seamless. It largely eliminates the need to unify the computer systems of the sender and recipient of customer data or to give the recipient full access to the sender's system, provided that certain common protocols are adopted to facilitate data exchange. From a technological perspective, this important 'plug-and-play' feature of modern data sharing platforms is predominantly enabled by APIs – sets of data standards, messaging formats and rules that allow different computer applications to communicate.[19]

Compared to data portability, data interoperability implies a closer integration between the information systems handling customer data. Whereas the former can give customers the ability to download their data once and later use it elsewhere at their discretion, the latter enables a 'continuous, interactive exchange' of data across systems.[20] In other words, interoperability makes the two systems *compatible* with one another.[21] Furthermore, to enable data portability, only one of the two information systems needs to be set up with export capability – but '[t]o become interoperable, *two* systems must consent to use the same protocols and exchange data.'[22]

Overall, *CDS 2.0* represents a major step forward from the first generation of legal frameworks for the sharing of customer data and seeks to overcome the main limitations of *CDS 1.0*.

First, as bespoke legal frameworks, different iterations of *CDS 2.0* can be free from the limitations of privacy laws. Their scope is not limited to personal information and can include data of business customers. While the more sophisticated privacy frameworks underpinning *CDS 1.0* may recognise in principle the right to data portability,[23] the exercise of that right can be limited by various restrictions, such as lengthy wait times to receive the requested data,[24] the need to comply with various conditions or obligations to consider the rights and freedoms of third parties.[25] Furthermore, *CDS 2.0* frameworks simplify the sharing process and enhance the usability of shared data through data interoperability. The latter complements data portability by addressing one of the main limitations of transferring data across different databases and transforms data portability from an abstract principle into a real enabler of better outcomes for customers who choose to share their data.

Second, *CDS 2.0* frameworks are sector-specific, which enables policymakers to adjust them to the risks of various sectors in the economy. In a sector-specific setting, legal certainty does not need to be sacrificed in favour of one-size-fits-all principles-based regulation: *CDS 2.0* regimes can implement bespoke data governance rules and technical standards developed specifically for the relevant sector.

Therein, however, lies the key limitation of *CDS 2.0* frameworks, which exist in the form of sectoral rules. In the next section we discuss the potential for applying the same mechanics to facilitate the sharing of customer data on a cross-sectoral, and even economy-wide, basis. This heralds the transition to the more advanced and ambitious third generation of customer data sharing frameworks – *CDS 3.0*.

1.4   *CDS 3.0*: multi-sectoral customer data sharing

While second-generation forms of *CDS* like open banking and open finance hold significant potential to disrupt the traditional 'silos' of customer data, their reach remains limited to just a single sector of the economy, namely finance. This limitation can be explained by pragmatism. After all, prioritising customer data sharing in finance is logical, since financial data tends to be more standardised, which in turn enables easier sharing of that data and subsequent processing. However, much of the potential of customer data remains unrealised, much of its value hidden in silos outside finance. It follows, as some experts argue, that open banking and open finance can be used as a launch pad for further expansion of access to 'all customer data, wherever it is held across all firms and all sectors' in order to 'enable customers to be empowered across all of their data, throughout the full breadth of the economy, and place all firms on a common footing of needing to support customer-elected data portability.'[26] The logic and reasoning underpinning open banking and open finance discussed in the previous section are even more powerful when extended into additional sectors, such as energy, telecommunications, pensions and even personal health services, and eventually economy-wide.

What to call this further expansion? The existing 'open banking'/'open finance' dichotomy underpinning *CDS 2.0*, which remains confined to a single sector of the economy, is clearly no longer sufficient. Hence, a sector-agnostic concept is needed to reflect an expanded coverage of customer data sharing which transcends sectoral limitations. In contrast to the twin concepts of 'open banking' and 'open finance,' which appear to be widely recognised and uniformly understood, there is no agreed term to describe the next stage in this evolution. To our knowledge, two options have received some support in recent years: 'open data' and 'smart data.' We find each unsatisfactory for the reasons explained below.

The phrase 'open data' is sometimes used in other contexts that are unrelated to the sharing of valuable customer-generated information discussed in this book – such as environmental statistics, government spending, healthcare, education and knowledge dissemination. In these sectors, 'open data'

refers to specific sets of data that are developed and shared in the public interest, rather than for the benefit of any one customer. As an example, these
data sets can promote visibility of government expenditure, help exercise
public control over socially important initiatives or facilitate the circulation of
knowledge generated by academic research. Ease of access to these types of
data determines their public benefit and explains why 'open data' is defined
more broadly in these specific contexts as data that 'can be freely used, modi-
fied, and shared by anyone for any purpose.'[27]

This interpretation of the term 'open data' makes it ill-suited to describe
the next stage in the evolution of *CDS* frameworks. Indeed, in the context of
sharing valuable customer data, unlimited publicity could be particularly detrimental to the customer. The reason is simple: the commercial value of most
customer-generated data largely lies in its non-public, often sensitive nature.
While consumers may appreciate transparent records of government spending
on healthcare and education, they are not likely to make their bank statements
or spending preferences publicly known. There are multiple instances where
customers may have a strong legitimate interest to have complete control over
how the data they generate is shared and who is permitted to access such data
(to the exclusion of everyone else). In this book, *CDS* refers to the sharing
of such customer data and therefore, by necessity, is a much more elaborate
multi-layered concept than facilitating *unrestricted* access to certain types of
data. It is concerned with preserving privacy and integrity of customers and
enabling wider sharing of such data if and when the customer desires – which
explains the complex interplay of different objectives of *CDS* frameworks
discussed in Section 1.6.

'Smart data' is the term used in the UK to describe an extension of the
right to data portability which 'enables consumers, if they wish, to simply
and securely share their data with third parties, to enable them to provide
innovative services.'[28] According to the UK government's public consultation
dedicated to this concept, the key features of 'smart data' are (i) immediate
provision of customer data by a data holder to a third-party provider, (ii) use
of prescribed technology – APIs – to share customer data, (iii) ongoing, rather
than one-off transfer of data, where appropriate, (iv) adoption of common
technical standards, data formats and definitions to enable interoperability
and (v) provision of product and performance data in addition to customer
data to boost innovation.[29]

Between 'open data' and 'smart data,' the latter is the better term, as it
is not widely used in other contexts and therefore is less likely to be misin-
terpreted. Nonetheless, as a defined term to describe an advanced form of
customer data sharing, 'smart data' is far from perfect. Its etymology remains
unclear: why does more efficient sharing of customer data become 'smart' if
the use of that data is noticeably absent from the list of key features of 'smart
data'? Furthermore, while 'smart data' could be used to describe a certain data

sharing model, it is not sufficiently flexible to distinguish between sectoral, cross-sectoral and economy-wide applications of that model.

In the absence of a satisfactory term to capture the different stages of development of customer data sharing, we follow our evolutionary approach and distinguish a third generation of *CDS* frameworks as follows:

> CDS 3.0 is sharing customer data stored within multiple sectors of the economy as the customer directs for use as the customer desires.

In line with the definitions of 'open banking' and 'open finance' in Section 1.3, our approach to *CDS 3.0* is technology-neutral, customer-focused and under-pinned by the twin notions of data portability and data interoperability. Technological neutrality makes our taxonomy resilient to advancements in data processing and management – as future iterations of *CDS* frameworks may be based on technologies far more sophisticated than today's APIs.

We use the scope and breadth of these frameworks' coverage as the key characteristics separating *CDS 2.0* from *CDS 3.0*, and our definition of *CDS 3.0* is intentionally open-ended to accommodate its different modes of implementation across the spectrum from (i) *CDS 3.0* in the narrow sense to (ii) economy-wide *CDS 3.0*. Narrowly interpreted, third-generation *CDS* refers to *any* expansion of customer-directed data sharing outside the initial (most likely financial services) sector of the economy. In contrast, economy-wide expansion represents the ultimate form of implementation of *CDS* across all relevant sectors enabling customers to direct their data as they choose, wherever it resides.

Conceptually, *CDS 3.0* is a pinnacle of evolution of *CDS* frameworks. However, the three generations discussed previously are not mutually exclusive. Indeed, *CDS 3.0* replicates *CDS 2.0* across multiple sectors, whereas the staples of *CDS 1.0* – privacy and competition laws – continue to coexist alongside the bespoke *CDS 2.0* and *CDS 3.0* frameworks. Each of the following generations thus complements the previous one, as shown in Figure 1.1.

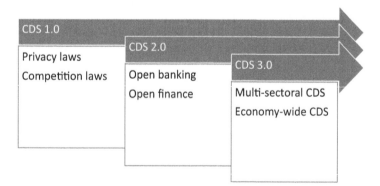

Figure 1.1 Evolution of CDS frameworks

We anticipate most *CDS 3.0* frameworks will progress gradually towards economy-wide implementation by integrating additional sectors over time. Australia's Consumer Data Right regime (introduced in Section 1.5) – the only *CDS 3.0* framework in the world in operation at the time of writing – is currently undergoing such transition, illustrated by Figure 1.2.

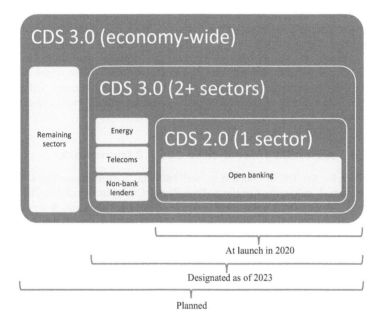

Figure 1.2 Transition from *CDS 2.0* to *CDS 3.0* in Australia

Notes: The 2023 data includes sectors that have been formally designated under Australia's Consumer Data Right framework. At the time of writing, the roll-out among non-bank lenders was only partially complete and put temporarily on hold in telecommunications to give the regime time to mature. See also Section 1.5.

While a coherent taxonomy of data sharing frameworks is important on its own, the separation of *CDS 3.0* into a separate category is necessary, since the expansion of *CDS 2.0* functionality across multiple sectors creates a noticeably different environment for customer data, along with *distinctive new risks* and *regulatory challenges.*

On the one hand, *CDS 3.0* creates new opportunities for market participants to develop more relevant use cases for customer data and eventually better consumer outcomes that are not limited by sectoral boundaries. Cross-sectoral *CDS* frameworks reduce (and at the economy-wide level effectively eliminate) gaps that may emerge when the same types of customer data end up regulated and shared differently depending on the type of entity which holds such data at the time. The most ambitious (economy-wide) implementation of *CDS* is thus better aligned with the commercial reality, which makes sectoral adjustments to the sharing of some data artificial and unnecessarily complex (due to inbuilt discrimination based on the origins of data). On top of that, a uniform *CDS* regime that spans multiple sectors may significantly boost adoption, particularly by the least sophisticated end-users like individual consumers, by reducing the need to deal with multiple concurrent legal frameworks for different types of customer data – each with different sectoral definitions, boundaries, regulators, intermediaries and data transmission specifics.

On the other hand, *CDS 3.0* presents very different regulatory challenges compared to isolated sectoral data sharing frameworks, which call for a different policy and regulatory response. These challenges will be the subject matter of subsequent analysis and are briefly summarised in Chapter 2.

1.5   Australia's world-first CDS 3.0 framework

Australia has led in conceiving, and building, a third-generation *CDS* framework called the Consumer Data Right (CDR). Introduced in 2020, the CDR empowers customers[30] in Australia to direct data which service providers hold about them to other providers of their choice so that these providers can offer a better value for money service.[31] The CDR regime gives customers the ability to exercise greater control of data once used by service providers for their own ends and requires the latter to unlock the 'silos' of customer data.

Crucially, the Consumer Data Right was from conception *designed as a multi-sector (and ultimately an economy-wide) framework*[32] and its initial implementation in the form of open banking was incidental and predicated on the ease of implementation in the heavily concentrated and regulated banking industry. Since its launch in 2020, the CDR has been extended to the energy sector,[33] as well as to non-bank lenders.[34] The proposed expansion to superannuation (pensions), insurance and telecommunications was paused in mid-2023, to allow the CDR ecosystem to mature and the quality of the data to be improved in finance and energy.[35] However, the clear message is that the slightly delayed broad roll-out across multiple sectors of the economy will in due course proceed.[36]

Upon its expansion beyond finance to the energy sector, Australia's CDR became the *first CDS 3.0 regime in the world*.[37] The Consumer Data Right is thus the prime source we draw upon for valuable insights into the mechanics, implementation and enforcement of third-generation *CDS* frameworks.

The CDR is a mandated statutory framework introduced into Australian law by several instruments: (i) the *Treasury Laws Amendment (Consumer Data Right) Act 2019* (Cth), (ii) the *Competition and Consumer (Consumer*

Data Right) Rules 2020 (Cth) (*CDR Rules*)[38] and (iii) the standards made by the Data Standards Chair, who is assisted by the Data Standards Body (DSB).[39]

The Consumer Data Right combines the features of data portability and data interoperability and facilitates the sharing of certain categories of customer data (CDR data) with the customer's consent using prescribed data transmission channels. This is achieved through the interaction between two groups of entities known as 'CDR participants'[40]: 'data holders'[41] and 'accredited data recipients'[42] (ADR). Data holders are the incumbent businesses which initially create and maintain the isolated 'silos' of CDR data and whose control over that data the CDR is meant to disrupt, while accredited data recipients are regulated entities authorised under the law to receive CDR data. Although the CDR enables the direct sharing of customer data between service providers, the more limited data portability is also recognised in principle and should be achievable through disclosures of CDR data directly to the customer[43]; however at the time of writing this 'export' functionality remains disabled.[44]

Since the types of data holders and CDR data are sector-specific, the CDR framework incorporates another type of instrument for added flexibility – sectoral designations. The latter facilitate the CDR's gradual expansion across different sectors of the economy and expressly identify the types of customer data covered by the framework. As an example, in the banking sector, CDR data includes various types of customer data, account data and transaction data relating to 29 different 'products' (from savings accounts and term deposits to overdrafts and trust accounts).[45] In addition, sectoral designations identify the data holders, which include authorised deposit-taking institutions[46] in the banking sector,[47] energy retailers and other prescribed entities in energy[48] and carriers and carriage service providers[49] in the telecommunications sector.[50]

The Consumer Data Right establishes technical data standards that prescribe the format of data, its method of transmission and translate into practice an extensive set of information security controls designed to protect consumer data from unauthorised access and misuse. To continue our analogy of *CDS* frameworks with sanitation systems from Section 1.1, these standards determine the design and composition of the data transmission channels (pipes) to make the flow of data safe and efficient. Stringent accreditation requirements seek to ensure the data (water) in the CDR's ecosystem is flowing between businesses that are trustworthy. The valve which determines whether data flows or not is consumer consent. Data holders must ask consumers to authorise disclosure of their CDR data and keep records of such authorisations. Businesses accredited to receive CDR data can only receive it with the consumer's consent. The CDR also performs an important hygiene function. When an accredited data recipient no longer needs CDR data and is not required to retain it, it must either delete it or effectively de-identify it. Consumers can also instruct deletion of CDR data.[51]

The operation of the Consumer Data Right is overseen by several regulators,[52] most notably the Australian Competition and Consumer Commission (ACCC), which acts as the Data Recipient Accreditor[53] and issues authorisations to prospective recipients of CDR data.

1.6   *CDS 3.0* objectives

The underlying objectives that govern post-*CDS 1.0* frameworks have been mostly discussed by reference to 'open banking' and 'open finance.'[54] However, as can be gleaned from the CDR in Australia, the Smart Data Initiative in the UK and the nascent Consumer Data Right regime in New Zealand, the objectives of *CDS 3.0* frameworks are closely aligned with those of *CDS 2.0*.[55] This finding is far from unexpected, given that, as we argue in this book, *CDS 3.0* regimes operating across multiple sectors or economy-wide constitute a logical progression of the concepts of open banking and open finance. Despite some differences in how *CDS 2.0* and *CDS 3.0* are currently shaped or implemented across the globe, four purposes are commonly asserted: the desire to promote competition, encourage innovation, serve customers and enhance customer protection. We address each of these objectives in turn.

1.6.1   *Promoting competition*

Many industries experience competition problems. The goal of improving competition has therefore been fundamental in many jurisdictions for developing *CDS 2.0* frameworks. For example, the revised Payment Services Directive (PSD2) that laid the foundation for open banking in the European Union stresses the need for and benefits of increased competition multiple times.[56] Aimed at enabling an efficient payment market that allows existing and new payment service providers to offer their services within a clear legal framework, PSD2 sees no space for unjustifiable discrimination against any market participants, regardless of their business size or model.[57]

In the UK – the pioneer of open banking in Europe – but also in Australia and elsewhere, the desire to promote competition between large, established financial institutions (incumbents) and smaller, newer banks and emerging financial technology firms (fintechs)[58] was one of the leading factors spurring the roll-out of open banking.[59] Because of the 'gatekeeper role' that the established banks have assumed with respect to their client data, they have long enjoyed a substantial advantage in providing financial services when compared to smaller banks and fintechs that had to vigorously fight to win their clients.[60] Even where new entrants were able to somehow gain a foothold in the market, high switching costs and network effects[61] perpetuated the situation where customers stayed 'locked in' with their banks even where new entrants offered superior products or services.[62] By 'opening' customer data residing with the incumbents for other financial service providers, open banking mitigates this information asymmetry problem and removes barriers for new market entrants. Many customers who may have been reluctant to leave their existing provider because of the actual or perceived difficulties associated with switching the accounts or finding a better product on the market are given the opportunity to select an alternative financial service provider that better suits their needs.

This simple rationale equally applies to many other economy sectors where customer data is kept within the businesses that originally collected the data. In fact, all three jurisdictions walking or preparing to walk the path of *CDS 3.0* have explicitly recognised the need for improved competition beyond banking and finance.[63] In sectors like energy, telecommunications, retail or travel, to name just a few, established service providers often have a firm grip on customer data allowing them to maintain a competitive edge over smaller, innovative companies. For example, retail customer data collected through loyalty programmes offers service providers valuable insights into customer behaviour, preferences and purchasing habits and allows them to tailor their strategies and offerings in ways that influence and shape customer choices, drive repeat purchases and increase customer lifetime value.[64] Comparable to the financial sector's situation, customers might be unwittingly 'locked in' even where superior alternatives exist. By facilitating the transfer of customer data from established retail providers to other service providers, the playing field becomes more level. This rectification of the information asymmetry problem not only dismantles barriers for new entrants but also empowers customers to turn to other providers.

When customers are empowered to control who can access their data and how their data is used, all industries are compelled to become more efficient and competitive.

Crucially, in promoting competition, second- and third-generation *CDS* frameworks equally restore a commercial morality – a fundamental fairness, that modern businesses often prefer to overlook.[65] Today, new customers are routinely offered by banks more favourable terms for financial products than existing customers. E-commerce platforms frequently tailor prices for potential purchases to individual customers based on various factors, ultimately resulting in lower-income customers often paying more for their purchases.[66] With the 'action initiation' functionality integrated in *CDS 2.0* and *CDS 3.0* frameworks (see Section 3.2) changing providers across relevant economy sectors could potentially be accomplished with just a few clicks on a mobile device. As a result, current providers will miss out on the opportunity to win back customers by providing a more appealing offer when they call to terminate their current contracts, as is the common practice outside *CDS 2.0* and *CDS 3.0.* Existing providers will be compelled to ensure fair treatment of all customers from the outset, or risk losing them irretrievably at any moment.

1.6.2   Encouraging innovation

Greater competition goes hand in hand with innovation. When faced with escalating competition from new market players capable of swift adaptation to customer requirements and offering more competitive pricing, incumbents are compelled to upgrade or modernise their outdated technology systems, potentially reorganise or rethink their business models, or at a minimum improve their product and service offerings.[67] Indeed, insights gained from customer data can enable service providers to understand individual customer needs and preferences and tailor their products and services accordingly (see also Section 1.6.3). Personalisation not only enhances customer satisfaction but also encourages innovation in designing unique offerings that cater to specific needs.

In recognition of this simple fact PSD2, for example, foresees 'the development of user-friendly, accessible and innovative means of payment.'[68] Similarly, the CDR seeks to create an environment for the growth of new ideas and businesses where data-driven innovation can thrive.[69] The emerging *CDS 3.0* regimes in the UK and New Zealand explicitly share this intention.[70] Ultimately, increased innovation across economy sectors helps industries adapt to changing circumstances, identify new opportunities and devise more efficient business practices thus also building up sectoral resilience.[71]

1.6.3   Serving customers and fostering inclusion

Second- and third-generation *CDS* regimes are customer focused. They go to those who control data.[72] As mentioned earlier, historically, service providers regarded customer data as their own with details of customer usage of products and services typically held and controlled by the service-providing entities.[73] Whenever customers wished to change service providers, they had to obtain the relevant information from their existing providers and forward it to potential competitors. Customers also had to verify that their data was compatible with the format used by competing providers. These data access and transfer processes were often hindered by the lack of a general requirement on data holders to furnish requested information in a standardised, portable and machine-readable form that could be promptly processed by other service providers chosen by the customers. Across many sectors, both public and private, customers were the sole authorised recipients of data with no mechanism for third parties to directly access relevant information from the customers' existing providers.[74]

The combination of data portability and data interoperability that characterise the second- and third-generation *CDS* frameworks profoundly change this situation. By enabling customers to instruct their providers to disclose relevant data to other providers of their choice in a fast and expedient manner, *CDS 2.0* and *CDS 3.0* assist customers in tracking their financial status, utilities or other needs, facilitating easier comparisons and transitions between various offerings.[75] Ultimately, *CDS 3.0* regimes should help customers move towards more sustainable and affordable lifestyles and enhance customer welfare.[76]

The *CDS 2.0* and *CDS 3.0* regimes may also facilitate inclusion: access to customer data allows service providers to deliver products and services to the market that speak to the needs of those who have been underserved or unserved by existing providers. The analysis of data on the consumption of utilities or telecommunication services, for example, may usefully inform the assessment of the customer's creditworthiness – a process traditionally reliant on financial data only and therefore less capable of revealing potentially valuable details on the customer's lifestyle.[77] While some governments have embraced open banking to improve financial inclusion, above all Mexico, Brazil and India,[78] this process would be enhanced by a broader *CDS 3.0* regime.[79]

1.6.4   Enhancing customer protection

Second- and third-generation *CDS* frameworks may pursue several customer protection objectives.

The foremost risk that such frameworks seek to address is insecure handling of customer data. Transaction data can unveil extensive information about an individual, including political affiliation (revealed through donations), health status (indicated by payments to healthcare providers), location and movement (discernible from spending patterns) and other personal details that can be inferred through expenditure analysis. This data can also facilitate identity theft.[80] Besides compromising privacy and potentially causing financial harm to customers, insecure storage or transmission of data equally puts at risk the reputation of data holders and recipients. As a result, their ability to attract new customers or form business partnerships suffers. To ensure both customer interest and customer trust in the use of *CDS 2.0* and *CDS 3.0* they must provide a safer and more reliable alternative to existing data sharing arrangements.

Having introduced standardised APIs for data transmission, open banking serves yet again as a case in point. Before open banking, the prevalent method of getting access to customer banking data was 'screen-scraping' – the practice whereby customers give their bank account login credentials to third parties who then 'scrape' data from the customers' internet banking interfaces and use it to offer financial products and services, in addition to or in lieu of the products and services offered by the customers' bank.[81] As will be explained in more detail in Sections 4.3 and 5.2.2, SS, while still in use in many jurisdictions, is a highly controversial practice which relies on a slow and unstable technology, exposes customers to significant cybersecurity risks and renders them an easy target for malevolent actors. In contrast, under open banking, customer login credentials are only known to the customers themselves and their bank which significantly reduces the risk of security breaches and has been a key factor in the adoption of open banking in India, the UK and the EU (and the decision by the Canadian government to launch open banking in due course).[82] In Canada, for example, the Advisory Committee on Open Banking lists protection of customer data as the first of six key customer outcomes that are expected to underpin the Canadian open banking system.[83]

Given that *CDS 3.0* frameworks significantly increase the number of entities that may be granted access to customer data, the potential risks associated with the security of that data also increase: each entity might have varying levels of information security measures in place, and any weaknesses in their systems could be exploited by malicious actors to gain unauthorised access to the sensitive customer information (see also Section 5.2.2). As each additional entity with access introduces a new potential point of vulnerability through which customer data could be compromised or misused, the objective of customer protection becomes even more prominent for *CDS 3.0* frameworks.

Ensuring safety of customer data lies therefore at the heart of the CDR which imposes detailed information security requirements, including an extensive set of minimum information security controls (see also Section 5.2.2).[84] The nascent *CDS 3.0* regimes in the UK and New Zealand equally emphasise the need to ensure secure handling of customer data, including that it be transferred through secure data transmission channels.[85] Second- and third-generation *CDS* regimes may also have other customer protection objectives, such as improving customer awareness and understanding of the risks and benefits of sharing their data across economy sectors. This aspect of customer protection has been strongly emphasised in Australia.[86]

While this section has addressed each of the objectives governing *CDS 2.0* and *CDS 3.0* frameworks separately, these objectives are not independent but rather are complementary and mutually reinforcing. A balanced implementation of all objectives is necessary to ensure that both *CDS 2.0* and *CDS 3.0* regimes mature as intended and thrive. Prioritising increased competition over customer protection, for example, risks making the system – which depends on customer participation – meaningless. Where customers have no or insufficient assurance that their data is treated safely, they are unlikely to participate in *CDS 2.0* or *CDS 3.0* (see Section 2.2).

1.7   *CDS 3.0* dynamics

While the objectives of *CDS 2.0* and *CDS 3.0* show hardly any variation, the dynamics of customer data sharing are noticeably different. Above all, a *CDS 3.0* framework shows much greater complexity even if the regime is structured as an 'umbrella' framework (similar to the design of the CDR) which helps in aligning its different components under a common vision and goal. In particular, as follows from Figure 1.3, the following variations to relatively simple *CDS 2.0* frameworks could be observed.

First, some economy sectors may require *different mechanics*, for example where different sets of data required for the provision of goods or services to customers are held by different entities. In the Australian energy sector, for instance, certain types of data are held by retailers (customer data, billing data, tailored tariff data, etc.) and other types of data (such as metering data or distributed energy resources register data) by the Australian Energy Market Operator (AEMO), an entity responsible for managing electricity and gas systems and markets across Australia. The latter is treated by the CDR as a 'secondary data holder' within what is called a P2P-model.[87]

Second, a 'gateway model' offers another example of how data flows may be organised within a *CDS 3.0* framework. Certain service providers may act both as data holders, but also as 'gateways' or 'pipelines' for the provision of customer data from other data holders to accredited recipients. The model is advantageous where it allows leveraging data sets already created and held by the 'gateway data holder' and saving costs for smaller retailers.[88] In fact, the initial CDR design for the energy sector envisaged that the AEMO would act as such a 'gateway data holder.' The model was later rejected, however, in favour of the P2P model for its enhanced interoperability and flexible infrastructure better positioned to support innovation and respond to potential cost and time constraints faced by the CDR participants.[89]

Third, customer data may be shared with unaccredited entities. Under the CDR, for example, such entities include 'trusted advisers' and 'representatives' (see Section 4.2). In contrast to 'trusted advisers' who – subject to customer request – receive customer data from an accredited person by virtue of belonging to a profession considered to be appropriately regulated to ensure a strong level of customer protection, 'representatives' require a contractual arrangement with an ADR (principal) who requests customer data from a data holder and transmits it to the representative to enable the latter to provide services to the customer.[90]

Fourth, different customers may be subject to different processes, some granting certain customers greater flexibility to choose the recipients of their data (as currently witnessed in Australia with the introduction of the classification of 'business consumers' who are empowered to share their own data with nearly whomever they choose, see Section 4.2.5).

Fifth, *CDS 3.0* frameworks are likely to introduce tiered levels of accreditation to ensure wide-scale participation by service providers and account for the risk factors associated with customer data sets, activities of the accredited persons and existing risk-mitigating measures (see also Sections 4.1 and 4.2).[91] Under the CDR, for example, two levels of accreditation exist: 'unrestricted' (which allows the service provider to collect customer data from both data holders and other accredited data recipients) and 'sponsored.'[92] Sponsored participants cannot collect customer data directly from the data holder. Instead, customer data is collected for them by their 'sponsors' who are unrestricted level participants.[93]

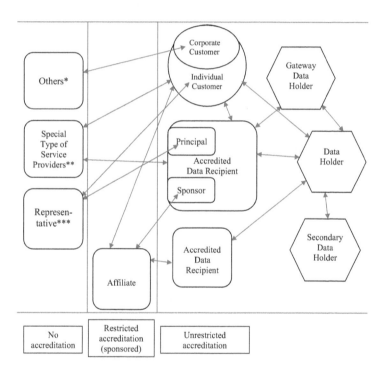

Figure 1.3 CDS 3.0 dynamics

Notes: * Note that under the CDR, only 'CDR business consumers' (i.e., corporate customers) can share data with nearly any service provider of their choice.
** Note that under the CDR, a special type of service providers are 'trusted advisers,' that is 'professions that are considered to be appropriately regulated to receive CDR data' (see Sections 4.2 and 5.2.1).[94]
*** Note that under the CDR, 'CDR business consumers' (i.e., corporate customers) cannot directly share their data with 'CDR representatives' (see Section 4.2).

Notes

1 Dan Awrey and Joshua Macey, 'The Promise and Perils of Open Finance' (2023) 40(1) *Yale Journal on Regulation* 1, 3.
2 Ibid.
3 See, e.g., Scott Farrell, 'Banking on Data: A Comparative Critique of Common-Law Open Banking Frameworks' (PhD Thesis, UNSW Sydney, 2022) iii.
4 See, e.g., *Tournier v National Provincial & Union Bank of England* [1924] 1 KB 461.
5 See, e.g., *Regulation (EU) 2016/679 of the European Parliament and of the Council of 27 April 2016 on the Protection of Natural Persons with Regard to the Processing of Personal Data and on the Free Movement of Such Data, and Repealing Directive 95/46/EC (General Data Protection Regulation)* [2016] OJ L 119/1 ('*GDPR*').
6 See, e.g., Anton Didenko, 'Cybersecurity Regulation in the Financial Sector: Prospects of Legal Harmonisation in the European Union and Beyond' (2020) 25(1) *Uniform Law Review* 125.
7 Multiple commentators have identified the existence of a 'small business' exemption as a deficiency in Australia's privacy laws. See, e.g., Attorney-General's Department (Cth), *Privacy Act Review* (Report, 2022) 52–4 <www.ag.gov.au/sites/default/files/2023-02/privacy-act-review-report_0.pdf>.
8 See Section 4.3.
9 See *Retail Banking Market Investigation Order 2017* (UK).
10 Scott Farrell, *Banking on Data: Evaluating Open Banking and Data Rights in Banking Law* (Wolters Kluwer, 2023) 3 ('*Banking on Data*').
11 Existing definitions of 'open finance' remain imprecise. As an example, Awrey and Macey define 'open finance' as 'the use of APIs [application programming interfaces] to promote information sharing between financial institutions, while simultaneously giving consumers more control over how their personal financial information is used and by whom': Awrey and Macey (n 1) 4.
12 Ibid.
13 See n 11. See also Francesco De Pascalis, 'The Journey to Open Finance: Learning from the Open Banking Movement' (2022) 33(3) *European Business Law Review* 397, 406–9: 'Open finance must be built with the same technology used in open banking, namely application programming interfaces (APIs)'; Emma Leong, 'Open Banking: The Changing Nature of Regulating Banking Data' (2020) 35(3) *Banking and Finance Law Review* 443, 444: 'Open banking involves sharing data with TPPs through application programming interfaces (APIs).'
14 'International Standard: Information Technology – Cloud Computing – Interoperability and Portability', ISO/IEC 19941:2017(E), standard 3.2.1 ('International Standard').
15 Note, however, that *CDS* frameworks can be designed to mandate that service providers share certain other types of data, such as data about products or services, as is the case in Australia. See Section 1.5; *Competition and Consumer Act 2010* (Cth) s 56AA(b) ('*CCA*').
16 Gabriel Nicholas, 'Taking It with You: Platform Barriers to Entry and the Limits of Data Portability' (2021) 27(2) *Michigan Technology Law Review* 263, 270.
17 Ibid.
18 International Standard (n 14) standard 3.1.1.
19 Daniel Jacobson, Greg Brail and Dan Woods, *APIs: A Strategy Guide* (O'Reilly, 2012) 5: 'An API is a way for two computer applications to talk to each other over a network (predominantly the Internet) using a common language that they both understand.'

20 Sukhi Gulati-Gilbert and Robert Seamans, 'Data Portability and Interoperability: A Primer on Two Policy Tools for Regulation of Digitized Industries' (Online, 9 May 2023) <www.brookings.edu/articles/data-portability-and-interoperability-a-primer-on-two-policy-tools-for-regulation-of-digitized-industries/>.

21 Nicholas (n 16) 271.

22 Gulati-Gilbert and Seamans (n 20) (emphasis added).

23 See, e.g., *GDPR* (n 5) art 20.

24 HM Government, *Smart Data: Putting Consumers in Control of Their Data and Enabling Innovation* (Report, June 2019) 11 <https://assets.publishing.service.gov.uk/government/uploads/system/uploads/attachment_data/file/808272/Smart-Data-Consultation.pdf> ('*Smart Data*').

25 See, e.g., *GDPR* (n 5) arts 20(1), 20(4).

26 Elevandi Insights Forum and National Australia Bank, *Open Finance and Beyond Roundtable* (Roundtable Note, 2023) 3 <https://web.archive.org/web/20230608144531/www.elevandi.io/wp-content/uploads/2023/02/Elevandi-Insights-Forum_Open-Finance-And-Beyond-Roundtable-Report.pdf>.

27 'Open Definition: Defining Open in Open Data, Open Content and Open Knowledge', *Open Knowledge Foundation* (Web Page) <https://opendefinition.org/>. See also 'Open Data Essentials', *The World Bank* (Web Page) <https://opendatatoolkit.worldbank.org/en/data/opendatatoolkit/essentials>.

28 *Smart Data* (n 24) 11.

29 Ibid.

30 Although the CDR framework uses the term 'consumer,' its definition is very broad and includes businesses: see Chapter 5. For simplicity, we will continue using the term 'customer,' except where the discussion references specific provisions of the Consumer Data Right regime which use the word 'consumer' or where the analysis distinguishes between different groups of customers, such as *individual consumers* in Section 5.2.

31 Note, however, that the CDR also regulates the sharing of other types of data, i.e., data about goods (such as products) or services that 'does not relate to any identifiable, or reasonably identifiable, consumers': *CCA* (n 15) s 56AA(b). The focus of this book is on the sharing of customer data rather than data about goods and services.

32 Explanatory Memorandum, Treasury Laws Amendment (Consumer Data Right) Bill 2019 (Cth) 5 [1.2] ('Treasury Laws Memorandum'): 'The Government has committed to applying the CDR to the banking, energy and telecommunications sectors, and eventually across the economy.'

33 *Consumer Data Right (Energy Sector) Designation 2020* (Cth).

34 *Consumer Data Right (Non-Bank Lenders) Designation 2022* (Cth).

35 Australian Government, 'Federal Budget' (26 May 2023) *Consumer Data Right Newsletter*.

36 Stephen Jones, 'Address to the Committee for Economic Development of Australia' (Speech, 7 June 2023).

37 At least in the narrow sense, as the CDR has not reached its economy-wide potential at the time of writing.

38 *Competition and Consumer (Consumer Data Right) Rules 2020* (Cth) ('*CDR Rules*').

39 See *CCA* (n 15) ss 56FH, 56FK.

40 See ibid s 56AL.

41 See ibid s 56AJ.

42 See ibid s 56AK.

43 See ibid s 56AA(a)(i).

44 For more detail, see Section 5.2.4.

45 See *CDR Rules* (n 38) sch 3.

46 See *Banking Act 1959* (Cth) s 9(3).

47 *Consumer Data Right (Authorised Deposit-Taking Institutions) Designation 2019* (Cth) s 5(2).
48 *Consumer Data Right (Energy Sector) Designation 2020* (Cth) s 12.
49 As defined in *Telecommunications Act 1997* (Cth) s 7.
50 See *Consumer Data Right (Telecommunications Sector) Designation 2022* (Cth) s 5(2).
51 See *CCA* (n 15) s 56BAA.
52 For more detail, see Chapter 7.
53 See *CCA* (n 15) ss 56CA, 56CG.
54 See, e.g., Treasury, Australian Government, *Review into Open Banking: Giving Customers Choice, Convenience and Confidence* (Report, December 2017) 8 ('*Review into Open Banking*'); OECD, *Shifting from Open Banking to Open Finance: Results from the 2022 OECD Survey on Data Sharing Frameworks* (Report, 2023) 13 ('*Shifting from Open Banking*').
55 Treasury Laws Memorandum (n 32) 5 [1.3]–[1.6]; *Smart Data* (n 24) 10; 'Consumer Data Right', *Ministry of Business, Innovation and Employment (NZ)* (Web Page, 18 August 2023) <www.mbie.govt.nz/business-and-employment/business/competition-regulation-and-policy/consumer-data-right/>.
56 *Directive (EU) 2015/2366 of the European Parliament and of the Council of 25 November 2015 on Payment Services in the Internal Market, Amending Directives 2002/65/EC, 2009/110/EC and 2013/36/EU and Regulation (EU) No 1093/2010, and Repealing Directive 2007/64/EC* [2015] OJ L 337/35, preamble, paras 4, 33, 51, 52, 67, arts 98(2)(c) ('*PSD2*').
57 Ibid preamble, para 33.
58 In this book, 'fintechs' are construed narrowly as a type of service providers that leverages innovative technology solutions to provide financial services and is distinct from incumbent financial institutions (e.g., banks).
59 Farrell, *Banking on Data* (n 10) 3–4; Treasury Laws Memorandum (n 32) [1.23], [1.45]; *Shifting from Open Banking* (n 54) 13.
60 See n 59.
61 On network effects, see Section 2.2.
62 Awrey and Macey (n 1) 26.
63 See *CCA* (n 15) s 56AA(c); *Smart Data* (n 24) 10; Customer and Product Data Bill (NZ) s 3(1)(b) <www.mbie.govt.nz/assets/exposure-draft-customer-and-product-data-bill.pdf> ('Customer and Product Data Bill').
64 ACCC, *Customer Loyalty Schemes* (Draft Report, September 2019) 34 <www.accc.gov.au/system/files/Customer%20loyalty%20schemes%20-%20draft%20report_151119.pdf>.
65 Natalia Jevglevskaja and Ross Buckley, 'The Consumer Data Right: How to Realise This World-Leading Reform' (2022) 45(4) *UNSW Law Journal* 1589, 1606.
66 Sung H Ham, Chuan He and Dan Zhang, 'The Promise and Peril of Dynamic Targeted Pricing' (2022) 39(4) *International Journal of Research in Marketing* 1150–1. See also Peter Stimpson and Alastair Farquharson, *Cambridge International AS and a Level Business Coursebook* (Cambridge University Press, 2014) 266.
67 Gustav Korobov, 'Open Banking as a World of Open Opportunities and Hidden Risks', *Finextra* (Blog Post, 12 June 2020) <www.finextra.com/blogposting/18875/open-banking-as-a-world-of-open-opportunities-and-hidden-risks>.
68 *PSD2* (n 56) art 98(2)(e).
69 Treasury Laws Memorandum (n 32) [1.23], [1.45].
70 *Smart Data* (n 24) 9–10; Customer and Product Data Bill (n 63) s 3(1)(b).
71 Harry Farmer and Madeleine Gabriel, *Innovation after Lockdown: Using Innovation to Build a More Balanced, Resilient Economy* (Report, June 2020) 14. See generally Mario Daniele Amore, 'Companies Learning to Innovate in Recessions' (2015) 44(8) *Research Policy* 1574.

72 Jevglevskaja and Buckley (n 65) 1603.
73 Awrey and Macey (n 1) 9, 22. See also Ben S Bernanke, 'Nonmonetary Effects of the Financial Crisis in the Propagation of the Great Depression' (1983) 73(3) *American Economic Review* 257, 263.
74 Productivity Commission, Australian Government, *Data Availability and Use* (Inquiry Report No 82, 31 March 2017) 194.
75 Treasury, Australian Government, *Strategic Assessment: Outcomes* (Report, January 2022) 13.
76 Jevglevskaja and Buckley (n 65) 1604.
77 Farrell, *Banking on Data* (n 10) 5.
78 Yan Carrière-Swallow, Vikram Haksar and Manasa Patnam, 'India's Approach to Open Banking: Some Implications for Financial Inclusion' in Linda Jeng (ed), *Open Banking* (Oxford University Press, 2022) 235; Ibid.
79 For example, Canada: see Advisory Committee on Open Banking, *Final Report: Advisory Committee on Open Banking* (Report, April 2021) 8.
80 ANZ, Submission to Productivity Commission, *Review into Open Banking in Australia* (September 2017) 22 [70] <https://treasury.gov.au/sites/default/files/2019-03/c2017-t224510_ANZ.pdf>.
81 *Review into Open Banking* (n 54) 51.
82 Farrell, *Banking on Data* (n 10) 6.
83 Advisory Committee on Open Banking (n 79).
84 *CDR Rules* (n 38) sch 2, pts 1, 2.
85 *Smart Data* (n 24) 28–9; Customer and Product Data Bill (n 63) ss 3(1)(c), 26.
86 Farrell, *Banking on Data* (n 10) 6.
87 Treasury, Australian Government, 'Peer-to-Peer Data Access Model in the Energy Sector: CDR Rules and Standards Design Paper' (Paper, 30 April 2021).
88 Grant Thornton, *CDR Gateway Model Review* (Report, April 2021) 6, 10.
89 Ibid 5.
90 Consumer Data Right, Australian Government, 'Accreditation Fact Sheet: Version 2' (Fact Sheet, December 2022) 12 ('Accreditation Fact Sheet').
91 Australian Government, *Inquiry into Future Directions for the Consumer Data Right* (Report, October 2020) 118.
92 Accreditation Fact Sheet (n 90) 3.
93 *CDR Rules* (n 38) r 7.4(2).
94 Ibid.

Chapter 2

Foundations of CDS 3.0 frameworks

Abstract

Chapter 2 examines the foundations of *CDS 3.0* frameworks by analogy with building a house – and considers three critical elements of that process: (i) *blueprints*, (ii) *boundaries* and (iii) *building blocks*. The '*blueprints*' in *Section 2.1* refer to the different regulatory approaches towards *CDS 3.0*, from voluntary and purely facilitative models to formal prescriptive legal frameworks. After examining the alternative approaches, the section argues that prescriptive regimes are better placed to address the risks of market concentration which *CDS 3.0* may well facilitate by giving rise to large technology platforms known as data aggregators. *Section 2.2* examines the legal *boundaries* of third-generation *CDS* platforms by analysing the complex relationship between them and competition, consumer, privacy and information security laws. Finally, *Section 2.3* provides a general overview of the key components (*building blocks*) of *CDS 3.0* frameworks, which are then analysed in greater detail in subsequent chapters.

2.1 Blueprints: benefits of a mandated regulatory framework

Should *CDS 3.0* regimes be mandated? The answer is likely to be 'it depends' with a range of factors playing a role in the decision-making process: the size and maturity of the data market, the scope and efficiency of the regulatory architecture, political foresight and others. While there are clear benefits to a mandated approach, alternative data sharing regimes also exist.

Presently, an increasing number of jurisdictions are adopting innovative customer data sharing practices in the banking and finance sectors and the trend is set to grow in number and scope.[1] Besides the EU, the UK and Australia, the list includes, for example, Brazil, Canada, Chile, China, Colombia, Hong Kong, India, Israel, Japan, New Zealand, Mexico, Philippines, Singapore, Saudi Arabia, South Africa, South Korea, Türkiye, United Arab Emirates, and the United States (US).[2] There is not a single prevailing approach: depending on policy objectives and economic conditions, current frameworks differ in terms of (i) the range of available services and products, (ii) the degree of standardisation (concerning, e.g., data security, messaging protocols

DOI: 10.4324/9781003414216-2

and interfaces), (ii) the role and type of regulatory and/or advisory bodies, (iv) timelines for implementation and (v) accredited data recipients.[3] Still, these diverse approaches can generally be categorised as: prescriptive[4] (where designated authorities regulate data sharing methods and oversee implementation), facilitative[5] (offering non-binding guidance and standards on the disclosure of data and its transfer), and market- or industry-led (offering no guidance or rules on customer data sharing).[6]

Most of the above jurisdictions have followed a mandatory, that is, prescriptive, approach.[7] Indeed, when there is no explicit legal requirement, incumbent data holders often have strong motives to refrain from sharing customer data (see Section 1.1). Banks and other data holders are highly unlikely to join a voluntary framework unless they know their competitors will also be part of that framework. Mandated systems thus, at a minimum, ensure requisite levels of participation on the part of incumbents, tackle the 'customer data bottleneck' and 'customer lock in' problems (see Sections 1.1 and 1.6) and lower the switching costs for customers. Crucially, prescriptive frameworks help achieve *CDS 3.0* objectives in a structured and transparent manner. Furthermore, judging by the uptake of open banking and open finance in jurisdictions where such frameworks are mandated, they promise to be more efficient than facilitative or market-led systems.[8] Such frameworks establish clear rules of the game for all participants and, importantly, ensure accountability of data recipients.[9]

The analysis of risks that may be hidden in industry-led customer data sharing frameworks tilts the scales even further in favour of prescriptive ecosystems. The open banking and open finance systems in the US serve as a telling example upon which Awrey and Macey rely to argue for a regulator-led approach to both regimes despite the challenges that a shift to that model from the current market-driven approach in the US may entail.[10] They reason as follows.

The financial services sector in the United States holds the position as the largest, most fragmented and highly diverse globally. It operates within the most complex regulatory framework, marked by a few federal agencies and numerous state regulators who supervise distinct but frequently overlapping segments of the financial services industry.[11] The extensive fragmentation poses significant challenges for financial institutions in creating the standardised APIs required to realise the potential of open banking and open finance.[12] As a result, in the absence of government intervention and common industry standards, standardised APIs have been mostly developed by a few large technology platforms known as data aggregators.[13] Serving as the connective tissue of the open banking and open finance ecosystems, these platforms have long been linking service providers (incumbent financial institutions, fintechs) and customers. While incumbents turn to data aggregators to leverage cutting edge technology and save the time and expense of entering into individual legal and technical customer data sharing arrangements with thousands of fintechs, fintechs rely on data aggregators to establish and manage technical connections to customer accounts held by incumbents and to collect, package and bring to fintechs the customer data. This allows fintechs to concentrate their efforts on the advancement of core products and services.[14]

Three key dynamics transpire.[15] First, as entities collecting, analysing and transmitting customer information data aggregators benefit from *economies of scale and scope*. *Economies of scale* means that the cost per unit of providing a service reduces with an increase in the volume of delivery. While the development of the technological platform to securely transfer and store customer data usually involves high fixed costs, collection and delivery of these data – once the platform exists – involves little or no variable cost. *Economies of scope* significantly amplify the benefits of scale in data aggregation, as oftentimes, the insights from the analysis of customer data facilitate the expansion into the markets previously controlled by the data aggregators' own clientele. The ability of a data aggregator to centralise and monitor customer's cash flows from various banks provides it with the competitive advantage in developing, for instance, personal finance management tools (PFMs) and targeting those products to specific customers.[16]

Second, data aggregation exhibits all the characteristics of so-called *'two-sided' markets* where two distinct user groups (the incumbents and fintechs) ultimately benefit from interacting through a common platform, that is, data aggregator. As explained previously, fintechs need data aggregators to access customer data held by financial institutions to offer their customers novel financial products and services. Incumbent institutions, too, rely on data aggregators' services to give their customers easy and secure access to the innovative products offered by fintechs. As should be expected, each user group favours access to platforms that attract the largest number of users from the other group generating so-called 'network effects.'

Third, data aggregation attracts the best API developers. In theory, open APIs allow any software developer to adhere to the protocols specified by a data aggregator, granting them access or the ability to 'write to' the respective open banking or open finance platform. Predictably, API developers tend to write to the APIs of data aggregators that have an established base of customers.

These dynamics are clearly troublesome, as they point toward inevitable market concentration.[17] The economies of scale and scope are projected to push data aggregators to make substantial investments in advancing their technological platforms. The most successful investors will gain access to more information, reduce per-user costs, and boost their capacity to provide products and services of superior quality. Because of the network effects of the two-sided markets created by data aggregation, market participants (including software developers) are likely to be attracted to the data aggregation platform due to its quality as well as its widespread use by other participants. Ultimately, as Awrey and Macey project, data aggregators can be expected to erect significant barriers to entry for new market participants if not their disappearance altogether.

Specifically, the effects of the extant market-driven data sharing architecture in the US will be different in the short and long term.[18] In the immediate future, connected by data aggregators, the open banking and open finance ecosystems might fulfil the potential of fostering increased competition, advancing superior financial products and services, and establishing a more robust financial system. In the long term, however, we should expect monopolisation of the financial services market by a small handful of data aggregators having significant influence over the flow of customer information. Crucially, this will lead the market to a scenario where data aggregators will 'recreate the informational vaults that Open Finance is designed to unlock, with data aggregators supplanting banks and other incumbent financial institutions at the apex of the financial system.'[19]

To escape this pitfall, Awrey and Macey advocate for (i) a stronger regulatory involvement, including the introduction of the licensing regime for data aggregators; (ii) a more proactive role in fostering the development of standardised APIs by the federal government; (iii) the imposition of a universal access requirement preventing data aggregators from denying access to their platforms by financial institutions, fintechs or their customers; and, crucially, (iv) 'the structural separation of data aggregation from finance, [to prevent] data aggregators from directly or indirectly offering financial products and services.'[20] It remains to be seen to what extent these recommendations will be taken on board by the US Consumer Financial Protection Bureau which in June 2023 announced its decision to regulate open banking by 2024.[21]

Certainly, given the business model of data aggregation and the growing economic stature of a few leading data aggregators, such as Plaid, Envestnet | Yodlee, Finicity and MX, the dynamics described above will only become stronger upon transition to *CDS 3.0.* Where data aggregation services move beyond banking and finance to other economy sectors, they not only reap the benefits of the economies of scale and scope in those sectors but also replicate two-sided market scenarios with the best API developers 'locked in' with the most influential data aggregators. Restated, in the long run, monopolisation of financial services by a few data aggregators will lead to them subsequently establishing a monopoly on the delivery of products and services in (many) other economy sectors if not across the entire economy. To illustrate, data aggregator's ability to consolidate, track and analyse customers' purchasing habits and participation in loyalty programmes in retail, tourism and entertainment will allow the data aggregator to develop more personalised products and services and more targeted marketing strategies. Providers previously established in those industries will forfeit their competitive advantage to data aggregators and new service providers will be robbed of any opportunity to establish their foothold in the market. We argue that this anticipated transformation in market dynamics and competitive landscape brings the advantages of a regulator-led model of customer data sharing clearly to the fore.

Still, the preference for alternative pathways for implementing open banking shown by a number of jurisdictions other than the US (such as Hong Kong, Singapore and Switzerland) proves that a strong regulatory involvement may not be regarded as the key enabler of an effective customer data sharing ecosystem. Rather, other factors (such as, for example, market and business autonomy) may be valued more and further, novel approaches may emerge in time. For example, the Canadian Advisory Committee on Open Banking 'firmly believes,' 'that neither an exclusively government led, nor industry-led approach is right for Canada'; instead, preferred would be 'a hybrid, made-in-Canada approach, one that harnesses the benefits of both industry and government-led models deployed elsewhere, but better reflects the Canadian context.'[22] It is possible that in developing their *CDS 3.0* frameworks other jurisdictions will emulate Canada's approach in relation to some or maybe even all economy sectors.

2.2   Legal boundaries of CDS 3.0

While mandated *CDS 3.0* frameworks offer distinct long-term advantages discussed in the previous Section, their integration into the legal system is not a trivial matter. As mentioned in Section 1.6, third-generation customer data sharing pursues multiple objectives at once: (i) promoting competition, (ii) encouraging innovation, (iii) serving customers and fostering inclusion and (iv) enhancing customer protection. In most legal systems, these objectives, when viewed in isolation from each other, are not unique and are likely to be dealt with at least partially by existing laws. This creates the boundary problem: the need to clearly distinguish *CDS 3.0 as a stand-alone legal framework* and in doing so avoid overlaps with pre-existing laws, such as competition laws, consumer protection laws as well as laws dealing with privacy and information security. Two important considerations follow from this.

On the one hand, a *CDS 3.0* framework does not need to be self-contained: policymakers should explore the feasibility of utilising the existing laws aligned with the *CDS 3.0* objectives to minimise overlaps. This is particularly relevant for *CDS 3.0* regimes which cover only a handful of sectors, rather than the entire economy, and thus effectively operate as an exemption from the otherwise applicable laws governing all other types of customer data. As explained further,[23] such restricted *CDS 3.0* frameworks may face particular difficulties when customer data enters or leaves the *CDS* ecosystem and thereby necessitates a transition between *CDS 3.0* rules and other laws governing customer data.

On the other hand, pre-existing laws may be poorly suited to meet the *CDS 3.0* objectives for a number of reasons. First, such laws may be insufficiently developed in the first place and thus lack the necessary functionality. As an example, this would be the case when privacy laws do not enable portability of customer data. Second, pre-existing laws may emphasise aims and principles that conflict with the *CDS 3.0* objectives. As an example, rules preventing disclosure of protected customer information may come in conflict with the competition rules aimed at facilitating broader access to customer data. In each of these scenarios, even non-mandated *CDS 3.0* frameworks would benefit from a bespoke enabling legal regime combining all the objectives outlined in Section 1.6.

We readily accept that each legal system is unique, and thus an attempt to draw universally accepted conclusions in this book would be futile. However, our focus on Australia's Consumer Data Right offers a unique opportunity to learn from the only fully implemented mandated *CDS 3.0* regime in force for several years at the time of writing.

As Sections 2.2.1–2.2.3 illustrate, the challenge of defining the boundaries of *CDS 3.0* is not a simple technical matter that is easily resolved by drafting *CDS* rules with sufficient precision to avoid textual overlaps with other laws. We argue that the relevant conflicts and overlaps with the existing laws may in some circumstances even undermine the utility of developing a bespoke *CDS 3.0* regime in the first place.

2.2.1 CDS 3.0 and competition law

Promotion of competition is a primary objective of *CDS 3.0* frameworks,[24] which seek to encourage service providers to develop products and services that better suit the specific needs and circumstances of individual customers. Australia's Consumer Data Right serves as a prime illustration. Here, the dominant role of competition promotion is recognised by scholars, who argue that 'the CDR has a clear policy priority predicated on the perspective of data portability as a competition law mechanism.'[25] This conclusion is supported by the structure of Australia's *CDS 3.0* framework, which was introduced into the law through amendments to the *Competition and Consumer Act 2010* (Cth) (*CCA*) rather than privacy legislation – in recognition that the *Privacy Act 1988* (Cth) 'has no clear *competition-enhancing* objectives'[26] and the privacy regulator (Office of the Australian Information Commissioner, 'OAIC') as the lead regulator 'could impair the *competition-enhancing* goals of the Open Banking system.'[27] These competition-enhancing goals extend beyond open banking to the entire CDR framework, which – aims – by enabling safe, efficient and convenient sharing of customer data – to 'create *more choice and competition*, or to otherwise promote the public interest.'[28]

As a special pro-competition legal regime integrated in Australia's *CCA*, the Consumer Data Right appears non-controversial. However, as discussed in Section 2.1, in contrast to the short-term positive pro-competition dynamics, in the long-term *CDS 3.0* frameworks may create strong incentives for market concentration and even monopolisation, presenting *novel competition risks* that need to be addressed. If not addressed by the *CDS 3.0* regime in a timely manner, these new risks may no longer remain self-contained and may effectively cross the boundaries of the *CDS* framework (as a limited pro-competition regime) and present new challenges to competition law as a whole.

The boundary issue becomes more pronounced if *CDS 3.0* is viewed through the lens of legal frameworks whose objectives may not be fully aligned with the objective of promoting competition. These include laws dealing with consumer protection, privacy and information security and are discussed below.

2.2.2   CDS 3.0 and consumer (protection) law

Consumer protection is a crucial part of *CDS 3.0* frameworks. As mentioned in Section 1.4, customers whose valuable data is shared through the *CDS 3.0* ecosystem, have a strong legitimate interest to prevent unrestricted sharing of such data and maintain control over how that data is shared. This legitimate interest needs to be protected – especially when the rights of *consumers*, the most vulnerable type of customers, are at stake – through the application of general consumer protection laws, or via the *CDS 3.0* framework, or both. Several boundary issues may arise as a result.

(a)   Consumer protection and promoting competition

A balance needs to be struck between the objectives of consumer protection and competition promotion. This is particularly important, considering the nuanced relationship between competition policy and consumer policy. On the one hand, the two 'speak the same language' since they 'share a common goal: the enhancement of consumer welfare'[29] – leading regulators around the world to seek cross-fertilisation between them.[30] On the other hand, despite obvious similarities, they are 'far from identical' as '[t]he two policies address this goal from different perspectives.'[31] Competition policy 'approaches a market from the *supply* side; its purpose is to ensure that through competition, consumers have the widest possible range of choice of goods and services at the lowest possible prices.'[32] In contrast, consumer policy 'approaches markets from the *demand* side: to ensure that consumers are able to exercise intelligently and efficiently the choices that competition provides.'[33] The result of these inherent differences is an intricate status quo whereby the two policies may occasionally come in conflict with each other: '[i]t often can be difficult to draw a clear distinction between a bona fide consumer protection initiative and an anticompetitive restraint.'[34] It follows that navigating a framework that pursues *both of these policies at once* is fraught with substantial coordination difficulties.

Sacrificing consumer protections to facilitate wider sharing of customer data may lead to unsatisfactory outcomes for several reasons.

First, consumer protection failures may generate lasting reputational risks for regulators and negative perception among end-users – particularly where the *CDS 3.0* framework is complex and therefore insufficiently understood.[35]

Second, some consumer protection failures cannot be effectively managed or remedied. As an example, if consumer data is intercepted by a cyber attacker (or another malicious actor), there is generally no way to retrieve the data (due to data's non-rivalrous nature). Simply put, once consumer data ends up in the hands of unauthorised recipients, it can be replicated and distributed to anyone without restrictions. As a result, damage to consumers resulting from a single data security breach could have long-lasting repercussions. This highlights the conceptual difference between customer data shared through *CDS 3.0* ecosystems and other kinds of valuable data, such as online banking account credentials: the value of the former lies in the information it contains, rather than in third-party actions based on that information. As an example, stolen online banking credentials have little value for the cyber attacker if the bank refuses to act on the hacker's instructions – which would be the case if the customer promptly notifies the bank about the cyber incident or if the bank's own fraud prevention measures detect an irregular account access pattern and block access to the customer's account.

Third, crucially, a strategy of promoting competition at the expense of consumer protection is, at core, short-sighted. After all, it can be rendered ineffective by market forces, such as long-term concentration risks of *CDS 3.0* discussed in Section 2.1. At the same time, damage to consumers can have long-lasting repercussions, including consumer mistrust and eventually apathy (see Chapter 5).

Fourth, we expect the number of participants in a *CDS 3.0* ecosystem to alter the relevance of each of the two regulatory priorities: as the number of participants increases, the more the focus will shift from efficiency towards safety (as system-wide or security failures will have a much stronger effect on consumer perception and trust).

(b)   Definition of 'consumer'

While consumer protection regimes routinely focus on the protection of particularly vulnerable groups of customers – such as individual consumers – *CDS 3.0* frameworks may apply to a wider range of customers, including businesses. This may create another boundary separating *CDS 3.0* regimes from 'general' consumer protection laws.

Australian law is a good case in point. Although the Consumer Data Right framework is part of the *CCA*, the former deviates substantially from the latter in its approach to defining a 'consumer.' The 'standard' definition of consumer in the *CCA* covers a limited range of persons: in particular, persons acquiring (i) goods or services intended for personal, domestic or household use or consumption,[36] (ii) goods or services costing up to a prescribed amount[37] or (iii) goods consisting of a vehicle or trailer acquired for use principally in the transport of goods on public roads.[38] While this definition may extend beyond *individual consumers*, it effectively focuses on the less sophisticated and potentially vulnerable customers that are likely to benefit from additional legal protections.

In contrast, the definition of 'CDR consumer' in the CDR framework is free from the above limitations[39] and covers all types of customers, be they individuals or businesses. It follows, somewhat strangely, that the legal framework entitled 'Consumer Data Right' is concerned with *all* types of customers, rather than consumers *stricto sensu*, as the concept is understood in Australian consumer protection legislation. The use of the word 'consumer' in the CDR's title thus appears almost incidental – as its meaning is analogous to the broad concept of 'customer' used in this book.

Until recently this oddity could have remained largely unnoticed. However, the 2023 revisions of the *CDR Rules* have attempted to distinguish business users among 'CDR consumers' to enable them to share their data more freely as more sophisticated customers. This was achieved by the introduction of a new concept of 'CDR business consumer' – a category covering CDR consumers that (i) are not individuals or (ii) have an active unique business identifier known as an Australian Business Number (ABN).[40] Strangely enough, there is no dedicated term to describe the remaining 'CDR consumers' – that is, individuals without an ABN – yet we expect this latter category of customers to be the primary beneficiary of consumer (protection) legislation, whether in Australia or overseas.

We also expect policymakers designing *CDS 3.0* frameworks in other jurisdictions will similarly evaluate the scope and reach of protections in general consumer protection legislation and determine whether the objectives of *CDS 3.0* will be better served by extending the framework to the sharing of data about (i) consumers as defined in domestic consumer (protection) laws,[41] (ii) non-consumers, (iii) combinations of (i) and (ii) subject to certain carve-outs or (iv) all customers without limitation.

We argue that *CDS 3.0* frameworks which apply to more sophisticated customers, as is the case in Australia, should incorporate additional protections for the most vulnerable customers, particularly individual consumers. Sections 5.2 and 6.1 outline several issues that may require such separation.

2.2.3 CDS 3.0 and privacy/information security law

While customers and service providers storing valuable customer data may pursue different objectives, both groups are motivated to limit third-party access to such data, albeit for different reasons. The latter are incentivised by the benefits of exclusive control (silos) of valuable data and are frequently subject to sectoral (e.g., banking confidentiality), privacy and information/cyber[42] security controls supported by regulatory penalties. Customers, on the other hand, seek to minimise the risks associated with data breaches – in particular, identity fraud.

CDS 3.0 affects both groups differently. It emphasises the role of customers' control over their data and at the same time strips away the benefits of exclusive access to data stored in the 'vaults' of data holders. As the overall dynamic shifts in favour of the customer, the relevance of privacy and information security rules is not diminished and increases even further – to match the increased risks of unauthorised access to customer data resulting from more frequent sharing of that data with third parties chosen by the customer. This raises the boundary issue: how should *CDS 3.0* frameworks interact with the existing privacy and information security laws? The answer is, inevitably, jurisdiction-specific, especially considering the different levels of maturity of relevant legal regimes among nations. As an example, some legal systems with sophisticated privacy laws may already enable portability of customer data[43] – whereas others will rely on customer data sharing frameworks to introduce data portability.

Our analysis of Australia's Consumer Data Right suggests that striking the appropriate balance between *CDS 3.0* and privacy laws can be particularly challenging due to the cross-sectoral nature of *CDS 3.0* frameworks.

In contrast to sectoral frameworks, like open banking or open finance, a *CDS 3.0* regime understandably requires a legal framework that spans multiple sectors. Assuming its gradual expansion to different sectors (as opposed to instant economy-wide roll-out, which we do not expect to be widespread), *CDS 3.0* will initially become an exception from the 'general' privacy regime. However, once it covers most of the economy, becoming the dominant framework for the sharing of customer data, then the status quo changes since the *exception becomes the norm*. For this reason, we argue, in the long-term domestic privacy legal regimes will need to adjust accordingly to reflect the key principles of *CDS 3.0*, thereby avoiding unnecessary duplication.

We now turn to Australia's Consumer Data Right to support our conclusions.

(a)   Consumer data right and Australian privacy principles

The relationship between Australia's Consumer Data Right and the *Privacy Act 1988* (Cth) is fraught with complexity. In contrast to the open banking frameworks in the European Union and the UK, Australia's CDR exempts customer data shared through it from the operation of the general privacy laws.[44] Instead, a bespoke set of privacy protections – known as 'Privacy Safeguards' – is integrated into the CDR framework 'to protect the privacy or confidentiality of CDR consumers' CDR data, whether the CDR consumers are individuals or bodies corporate.'[45]

While the CDR's Privacy Safeguards are modelled on the Australian Privacy Principles (APPs), which form the staple of Australia's general privacy legislation, the former completely override, rather than supplement the latter.

This is crucial: through the Privacy Safeguards, Australia's *CDS 3.0* framework 'effectively implements a new information privacy law regime.'[46] In simplified terms, this new privacy regime applies to CDR data once it is shared through the *CDS 3.0* framework but not before that.[47] In practical terms, this means that the same customer data is governed by (i) the APPs when it is in the hands of original data holders (such as banks) and (ii) the CDR Privacy Safeguards when it is transferred by the data holder to an accredited data recipient. One regime 'switches on,' the other 'switches off.'

The practical challenge underlying this switching process lies in the 'conceptually different structures' underpinning the two regimes: the *Privacy Act 1988* (Cth) is principles-based and 'provides a significant degree of leeway to the implementing bodies about how regulatory values and guidelines are implemented,'[48] whereas the Privacy Safeguards are prescriptive and highly specific. This produces a *two-track system for the same customer data*, which may 'lead to confusion on the part of regulated entities, who must switch between accorded discretion to implement broad privacy principles and following specifically prescribed rules and standards.'[49]

At the time of writing, Australia's Consumer Data Right has not yet achieved the status of the dominant framework for the transfer of customer data. However, as discussed earlier in this section, we argue that the duplication of privacy regimes will be unnecessary as the *CDS 3.0* regime matures and applies to other sectors, at which stage we expect the general privacy laws to evolve to the higher standards of *CDS 3.0*. The added benefit of this evolution is the increased legal certainty stemming from the more descriptive CDR framework.

(b)   Consumer data right and different levels of information security

A different kind of duality underpins the boundary issue between the Consumer Data Right and information security controls applicable to service providers storing customer data. The introduction of the CDR in Australia has resulted in the application of different rules to the same customer data (i) when it moves within the CDR ecosystem – and (ii) when it leaves that ecosystem. Notably, the duality of information security controls here is artificial: the *same* customer data is treated differently depending on its recipient.

At the core of this odd status quo lies the concept of 'trusted advisers' introduced into the CDR regime shortly after launch. 'Trusted advisers' is a collective term representing several groups of professional advisers (including accountants, lawyers, tax and financial advisers and mortgage brokers)[50] empowered to receive CDR data without obtaining CDR accreditation (which is required from other recipients) or oversight from the CDR supervisory authorities.[51] The reasons behind this are discussed in Section 4.2. For the purposes of this section, however, it is sufficient to acknowledge that trusted advisers occupy a privileged position among the third parties not formally included in the CDR ecosystem due to their exclusive right to receive a wide range of CDR data (including the data relating to *individual* customers).

Since trusted advisers are not subject to the CDR information security controls, the Explanatory Statement which accompanied the 'trusted adviser' reforms, sought to alleviate potential concerns by claiming that 'the minimum information security control of encrypting data in transit applies to the disclosure'[52] to a trusted adviser. A closer look at the CDR mechanics, however, reveals that the CDR's information security controls apply differently to CDR data *at rest* and *in transit*. Accredited data recipients must '[i]mplement robust network security controls to help protect data *in transit*, including . . . encrypting data in transit and authenticating access to data.'[53]

It follows that the CDR's information security provisions retain residual application only to the *process* of sharing CDR data with trusted advisers by ADRs, which is largely a *side effect* from the regulated status of accredited data recipients that transfer such data. These security controls cease to apply once the relevant data has reached its destination – and is *at rest* with the trusted adviser.

We argue that this status quo is unfortunate and calls for a response not limited to adjusting the internal mechanics of Australia's *CDS 3.0* regime. An efficient response should not discriminate against the same data based on its origins or destination – and lies in raising the level of protection *for all kinds of valuable customer data economy-wide*.

The cross-sectoral nature of *CDS 3.0* invites a rethinking of the scope of data protection frameworks. In finance, the role of information security is certainly paramount. After all, in the modern digital economy financial institutions that cannot protect their own computer systems cannot be trusted with client money. The same is true for digital assets[54] which typically operate outside the 'formal' financial system[55] and likely hold no value whatsoever if the databases housing them can be easily breached. But what about other, non-financial customer data? We argue there are valid reasons to extend the higher standard of protection to it as well.

First, *all customer data (and not just financial data) is valuable data*[56] – regardless of having easily ascertainable monetary value. This economic value explains the incentives of incumbents to control the 'silos' of customer data (as discussed in Section 1.1) and the expectation of increased market competition underpinning *CDS 2.0* and *CDS 3.0* (see Sections 1.3–1.4).

Second, stolen valuable data can be copied and reused multiple times, which may cause *long-term implications* for customers, including identity fraud.[57] It follows that customers may treat the security of such data as being as important as the *security of their money*. Once this is accepted, we argue, the law should seek to always protect such data – even when it is shared outside the *CDS 3.0* ecosystem.

Evening out the level of protection of valuable customer data across the economy is, admittedly, no small task. Nonetheless, it is fully aligned with the task of expanding *CDS 3.0* frameworks across different sectors of the economy: the greater the coverage of *CDS 3.0*, the more feasible the ultimate transition to a more secure economy-wide data protection standard.

We argue this process should integrate additional protections for *individual consumers* in the light of their more vulnerable position compared to other types of customers and general lack of specialist data security expertise. These additional protections could include a *closed list of prescribed channels for transmitting valuable consumer data to and from any entities (except between individual consumers)*,[58] which would affect service providers without restricting the freedom of individuals to share valuable data among themselves.[59]

Extending the level of customer data protection proposed above generates a range of benefits for the *CDS 3.0* ecosystem.

First, if for some reason the expansion of *CDS 3.0* to different sectors of the economy is delayed, the boundary issues discussed previously will lose their relevance: the gap between the higher *CDS 3.0* standards and the general information security requirements will be eliminated. In the context of Australia's CDR, this means trusted advisers will need to comply with the higher information security standard. As an added benefit, customer data will also *enter* the CDR ecosystem (by coming into possession of data holders) only via secure data transmission channels.

Second, a unified economy-wide approach reduces the opposition from unaccredited recipients of customer data who might otherwise resist their integration into the *CDS 3.0* ecosystem. In Australia, trusted advisers raised such objections on the basis that the Consumer Data Right should not interfere with their long-standing relationship with consumers:

> This is a relationship between the consumer and their trusted adviser, the CDR regime should not disrupt a relationship that has worked amongst the consumer and their trusted advisers for many decades.[60]

We expect this opposition to be much weaker if the unification is part of an economy-wide initiative to raise customer protection standards which effectively eliminates the first mover problem. In addition, our proposal does not negatively impact those professional advisers which already use secure data transfer channels (as they should) – it is meant to raise the level of information security of their less sophisticated counterparts.

Third, the proposed change is well aligned with the new programmes seeking to modernise and strengthen national information security frameworks. In Australia, this involves alignment with the strategic priority of the government to boost the level of information security nationwide.[61]

Fourth, as further elaborated in Section 5.2.2, the resulting reduction in the overall level of regulatory complexity mitigates the negative effects of limited consumer awareness of the relevant information security risks associated with the wider sharing of customer data. The multiple extensions of Australia's

Consumer Data Right to additional sectors, each with their own definitions, designations and data transmission specifics, are a good illustration of the self-perpetuating complexity of gradually expanding *CDS 3.0* frameworks. Considering that few consumers are fully aware of the extent of the relevant risks, the proposed unification reduces the instances of switching between different information security regimes and ensures the parties trusted by consumers remain trustworthy.[62]

Fifth, from a practical standpoint, the proposed approach will generate spillover benefits for the businesses handling customer data by eliminating the need to treat the same data differently depending on its origin. As an illustration, in Australia, recipients of customer data from different sources, only some of which are part of the CDR ecosystem, 'need to carefully design . . . consent flows and consider the impression [they] create in [their] interactions with consumers, to ensure [they] comply with the CDR framework and are not likely to mislead consumers.'[63] To ensure compliance with their CDR obligations, including the prohibition on misleading and deceptive conduct, businesses are faced with two options: (i) prevent co-mingling of CDR data with non-CDR data through careful strategic planning for the purposes of handling the *same* data, or, if co-mingling is hard to prevent reliably, (ii) protect *all* consumer data according to a CDR standard. Compliance is crucial, since co-mingling 'will not excuse [such businesses] from applying the high standard of protection that applies to CDR data.'[64] It follows that the boundary issue is likely to force many businesses into adopting the higher (*CDS 3.0*) standard anyway, and from this perspective our proposal does not appear to be such a radical departure from the status quo.

Lastly, achieving a high degree of harmonisation of information security controls across the economy is an important prerequisite for enabling disclosures of CDR data directly to the customer. As discussed in Section 5.2.4, at the time of writing this function of Australia's CDR framework (sometimes referred to as 'direct to consumer' data sharing) remained switched off for reasons such as inadequate protections for shared data.

(c)   CDS 3.0 *as a stepping stone towards modernising privacy and information security laws*

The above discussion suggests that the boundary issue in its different forms creates powerful incentives for adopting economy-wide *CDS 3.0* frameworks that facilitate *equal* treatment of the *same* data regardless of its origin or destination. Yet, if the end result is an economy-wide framework for all kinds of valuable customer data, one may begin to wonder whether the concept of 'customer data sharing' will at some point become redundant. While this sounds like a plausible hypothesis, we argue that *CDS* frameworks are likely to remain relevant for a long time for at least three reasons.

First, regardless of the degree of harmonisation of privacy and information security laws, the key function of regulated *CDS* regimes is to break open the 'silos' of customer data held by incumbents by mandating data holders to share such data as instructed by the customer. Without this compulsion, even fully harmonised data protection frameworks offer few benefits, since data holders may simply choose to keep the data to themselves.

Second, it is unlikely that all the boundary problems outlined in this chapter will be addressed simultaneously, as they require revisions of competition, privacy and information security laws. Furthermore, in the unlikely event this happens, the long-term, anti-competitive mechanics of *CDS 3.0* discussed in Section 2.1 may require further revisions to deal with the new risks.

Third, *CDS 3.0* frameworks can be used as a 'testing laboratory' for new data sharing rules before extrapolating them to the rest of the economy. The history of development of Australia's Consumer Data Right supports this view. After all, the CDR regime was meant to enhance the protections of customer data,[65] by integrating detailed information security obligations and ways to enforce those obligations upon breach.[66]

In Australia, the early signs of this transformation can already be observed in the Privacy Act Review Report published by the Attorney-General in February 2023[67] which set out several proposals for the modernisation of federal privacy laws. Some of the proposed reforms, if implemented, would bring the privacy laws into greater alignment with the Consumer Data Right (e.g., by empowering customers to enforce their rights more easily)[68] and help mitigate the 'trusted adviser' boundary problem by eliminating some of the legislative gaps that enable some trusted advisers (e.g., small businesses) to evade the application of the *Privacy Act 1988* (Cth).[69] Despite these early proposals, full alignment remains a very distant possibility. Nonetheless, as the Consumer Data Right gains momentum and covers additional sectors of Australia's economy, we argue that our more ambitious proposals (e.g., prescribing specific data transmission channels to share valuable customer data to or from non-individuals) could apply *only to CDR data* at first. After a period of testing in the *CDS 3.0* ecosystem, the new approach could be extended to *all valuable customer data*.[70]

2.3   Building blocks for *CDS 3.0* frameworks

There is no accepted blueprint for building *CDS 3.0* frameworks: at the time of writing, even the much simpler *CDS 2.0* (e.g., open banking) regimes have not yet become mainstream. Designing an efficient *CDS 3.0* framework requires careful balancing of different objectives outlined in Section 1.6 (some of which may conflict with each other) and addressing the boundary challenges discussed in Section 2.2. What other considerations are vital for policymakers? In this section, we briefly outline the key 'building blocks' towards *CDS 3.0*. These building blocks are then discussed in greater detail in the remaining chapters of this book.

Chapter 3 (Scope: expansion of the framework and write access)

Defining the scope of the framework is a crucial first step towards *CDS 3.0*. This building block affects how the *CDS 3.0* regime is structured (as a gradually expanding model or as an economy-wide initiative) and what the process of developing and sustaining an effective and efficient *CDS 3.0* could look like. It also involves identifying and understanding the main factors preventing wider adoption of *CDS 3.0* (such as the lack of action initiation, otherwise known as 'write access'), as well as the features of *CDS 3.0* that may improve its long-term viability (such as cross-border connectivity to link national *CDS 3.0* frameworks).

Chapters 4 (Service provider perspective: the quest for greater participation) and 5 (Customer perspective: the quest for customer trust)

The key enablers and users of *CDS 3.0* frameworks are the service providers which facilitate the exchange of customer data and the customers whose data circulates within the *CDS 3.0* ecosystem. We consider these two groups of stakeholders separately.

First, we establish the main factors affecting the motivation of service providers to participate in *CDS 3.0*, including the challenges and costs of accreditation, the existence of viable alternative pathways for sharing customer data that may compete with the *CDS 3.0* regime, the desirability of legal certainty and the competing interests of holders of customer data and prospective recipients.

We then proceed to discuss the customer's perspective. We establish customer trust as the key factor impacting customer participation in *CDS 3.0* frameworks and identify five enablers of customer trust: (i) accreditation, (ii) information security and privacy, (iii) customer redress, (iv) customer empowerment and (v) customer experience and awareness.

Chapter 6 (Enforcement: efficiency and fairness)

Enforcement is a critical component of *CDS 3.0* frameworks which pits the different stakeholders against each other and enables us to evaluate how the interests of these stakeholders are balanced and whether the resulting status quo is acceptable. We explain why ease of enforcement of customer rights is crucial in a *CDS 3.0* ecosystem and highlight the limitations of relying on mandatory insurance as a regulatory tool to boost customer confidence in *CDS 3.0*.

Chapter 7 (Regulation: oversight and flexibility)

Development of an appropriate oversight structure is vital for a *CDS 3.0* regime, considering the many competing objectives, risks and stakeholders.

We argue that *CDS 3.0* frameworks should remain agile and responsive to emerging and unexpected risks and should not be constrained by sectoral limitations. We also tackle the challenging issue of identifying appropriate performance metrics and evaluation criteria for *CDS 3.0* frameworks.

Chapter 8 (Conclusions: twelve lessons for the world)

We conclude our analysis by formulating 12 key lessons for the development of *CDS 3.0* frameworks informed by the discussion in Chapters 1 through 7.

Notes

1 See CBI and PWC, *The Global Open Finance Report* (Report, 23 March 2023) 19. See also The Paypers, *Open Banking Report 2019: Insights into the Global Open Banking Landscape* (Report, 25 September 2019) 10–8 <https://thepapers.com/reports/the-open-banking-report-2019-insights-into-the-global-open-banking-landscape-2/r780814>.

2 See CBI and PWC (n 1) 19; OECD, *Shifting from Open Banking to Open Finance: Results from the 2022 OECD Survey on Data Sharing Frameworks* (Report, 2023) 8–40 ('*Shifting from Open Banking*'). See also Oana Ifrim, 'Open Banking: A Very Global Business', *The Paypers* (Web Page, 19 December 2019) <https://thepapers.com/expert-opinion/open-banking-a-very-global-business-1240033>.

3 See Deloitte, Submission to Treasury, *Inquiry into Future Directions for the Consumer Data Right* (21 May 2020) 12–3.

4 Followed, for example, by Brazil, Colombia, EU, UK, and Australia.

5 Adopted, for example, by Hong Kong, Singapore, South Korea, and Japan. See Basel Committee on Banking Supervision, *Report on Open Banking and Application Programming Interfaces* (Report, November 2019) 10.

6 Followed, for example, by Switzerland and, at the time of writing, the US. See *Shifting from Open Banking* (n 2) 10.

7 Ibid 11.

8 See, e.g., Scott Farrell, *Banking on Data: Evaluating Open Banking and Data Rights in Banking Law* (Wolters Kluwer, 2023) 13.

9 See, e.g., Scott Farrell, 'Embedding Open Banking in Banking Law: Responsibilities, Performance, Risk and Trust Performance, Risk and Trust' (2022) 17(2) *Journal of Business & Technology Law* 265.

10 Dan Awrey and Joshua Macey, 'The Promise and Perils of Open Finance' (2023) 40(1) *Yale Journal on Regulation* 1.

11 Dan Awrey and Kathryn Judge, 'Why Financial Regulation Keeps Falling Short' (2020) 61(1) *Boston College Law Review* 2295, 2318–9.

12 Awrey and Macey (n 10) 5, 19.

13 In this book, 'data aggregators' are service providers that focus on the provision of data aggregation services to fintechs and other service providers (including incumbent financial institutions).

14 Ibid 5, 15.

15 Ibid 38–43.

16 By bringing together banking data from a variety of providers used by a customer, along with publicly available data about the range of financial products that customers might be interested in, PFMs are designed to give customers a more holistic view of personal finances, keep track of expenses, identify options for savings, etc.

17 Awrey and Macey (n 10) 38.

18 Ibid 6, 50.

19 Ibid 6.
20 Ibid 6.
21 See Rohin Chopra, 'Laying the Foundation for Open Banking in the United States', *CFPB* (Blog Post, 12 June 2023) <www.consumerfinance.gov/about-us/blog/laying-the-foundation-for-open-banking-in-the-united-states/>.
22 Advisory Committee on Open Banking, *Final Report of Advisory Committee on Open Banking* (Report, April 2021) 4, 25 <www.canada.ca/content/dam/fin/consultations/2021/acob-ccsbo-eng.pdf>. It remains to be seen, however, whether and to what extent the Canadian pathway will differ from the 'facilitative' approach.
23 See Sections 2.2.3, 4.2 and 5.2.
24 See Section 1.6.
25 Mark Burdon and Tom Mackie, 'Australia's Consumer Data Right and the Uncertain Role of Information Privacy Law' (2020) 10(3) *International Data Privacy Law* 222, 223.
26 Treasury, Australian Government, *Review into Open Banking: Giving Customers Choice, Convenience and Confidence* (Report, December 2017) 16 (emphasis added).
27 Ibid (emphasis added).
28 *Competition and Consumer Act 2010* (Cth) s 55AA(c) ('*CCA*').
29 OECD, *The Interface between Competition and Consumer Policies* (Executive Summary of a Policy Roundtable, 2008) 8 <www.oecd.org/daf/competition/40898016.pdf>.
30 Ibid 238.
31 Ibid 8.
32 Ibid (emphasis added).
33 Ibid (emphasis added).
34 Ibid 238.
35 The problem of insufficient customer awareness is discussed at Section 5.2.5.
36 *CCA* (n 28) s 4B; *Competition and Consumer Act 2010* (Cth) sch 2, ss 3(1)(b), 3(3)(b) ('*ACL*').
37 *CCA* (n 28) s 4B; *ACL* (n 36) ss 3(1)(a), 3(3)(a). At the time of writing, the prescribed amount for the purposes of acquisition of goods has been increased from AUD40,000 to AUD100,000: see *Competition and Consumer Regulations 2010* (Cth) r 77A.
38 *CCA* (n 28) s 4B; *ACL* (n 36) s 3(1)(c).
39 Section 56AI(4) of the *CCA* (n 28) disapplies Section 4B.
40 *Competition and Consumer (Consumer Data Right) Rules 2020* (Cth) r 1.10A(9) ('*CDR Rules*').
41 It is noteworthy that other legal systems may adopt a narrower definition of consumer (e.g., covering only individuals).
42 For a more detailed analysis, see, e.g., Anton Didenko, 'Cybersecurity Regulation in the Financial Sector: Prospects of Legal Harmonisation in the EU and Beyond' (2020) 25(1) *Uniform Law Review* 125.
43 For example, article 20 of the *GDPR* enables individuals to require the transfer of their personal information in a 'structured, commonly used and machine-readable format.'
44 Burdon and Mackie (n 25) 227.
45 See *CCA* (n 28) pt IVD div 5 ('Privacy safeguards') s 56EA.
46 Burdon and Mackie (n 25) 227.
47 For a more detailed explanation of the complex interplay between the APPs and Privacy Safeguards, see OAIC, *Consumer Data Right: Privacy Safeguard Guidelines* (Guidelines, November 2022) 10 <www.oaic.gov.au/__data/assets/pdf_file/0013/24034/Privacy-Safeguard-Guidelines-v4-Nov-2022-rev2.pdf>.
48 Burdon and Mackie (n 25) 233.

49 Ibid.
50 These are discussed in greater detail in Section 4.3.
51 But see Section 4.2.5 explaining a new accreditation exemption for recipients of business customer data.
52 Explanatory Statement, *Competition and Consumer (Consumer Data Right) Amendment Rules (No 1) 2021* (Cth) 20.
53 See *CDR Rules* (n 40) sch 2 pt 2 cl 2.2 (emphasis added).
54 For a comprehensive discussion, see, e.g., Ross Buckley, Anton Didenko and Mia Trzecinski, 'Blockchain and Its Applications: A Conceptual Legal Primer' (2023) 26(2) *Journal of International Economic Law* 363.
55 Anton Didenko and Ross Buckley, 'The Evolution of Currency: Cash to Cryptos to Sovereign Digital Currencies' (2019) 42(4) *Fordham International Law Journal* 1041.
56 For a more detailed analysis supporting this argument, see, e.g., Scott Farrell, 'Banking on Data: A Comparative Critique of Common-Law Open Banking Frameworks' (PhD Thesis, UNSW Sydney, 2022).
57 See, e.g., Keith B Anderson, Erik Durbin and Michael A Salinger, 'Identity Theft' (2008) 22(2) *Journal of Economic Perspectives* 171.
58 For more details, see Anton Didenko, 'New Ways to Reinforce Consumer Trust in Australia's Consumer Data Right' (2024) 50(1) *Monash University Law Review* (forthcoming).
59 The implications of limited customer expertise in the context of *CDS 3.0* are discussed in Section 5.3.4 above.
60 CPA Australia et al., Submission to Treasury, *Consumer Data Right Rules Amendments (Version 3)* (30 July 2021) 4 <https://treasury.gov.au/sites/default/files/2021-10/charteredaccountants.pdf>.
61 See Australian Government, *Australia's Cyber Security Strategy 2020* (Report, 2020) <www.homeaffairs.gov.au/cyber-security-subsite/files/cyber-security-strategy-2020.pdf>; 'Uplifting Data Security across Australia', *Department of Home Affairs (Cth)* (Web Page, 30 May 2023) <www.homeaffairs.gov.au/reports-and-publications/submissions-and-discussion-papers/data-security>.
62 The implications of consumer trust in *CDS 3.0* frameworks are discussed in Chapter 5.
63 'Guidance on Screen-Scraping', *Consumer Data Right* (Web Page, 25 March 2021) <https://cdr-support.zendesk.com/hc/en-us/articles/900005316646-Guidance-on-screen-scraping>.
64 Ibid.
65 See Treasury, Australian Government, *Consumer Data Right Privacy Protections* (Report, December 2018) 4 <https://treasury.gov.au/sites/default/files/2019-03/CDR-Privacy-Summary.pdf>.
66 Ibid.
67 Attorney-General's Department, Australian Government, *Privacy Act Review* (Report, 2023) <www.ag.gov.au/sites/default/files/2023-02/privacy-act-review-report_0.pdf>.
68 See proposal 26.1 to give individuals 'a direct right of action . . . to apply to the courts for relief in relation to an interference with privacy': Ibid.
69 See proposal 6.1 envisaging the conditional removal of the 'small business exemption': Ibid.
70 This can be achieved, e.g., through amendments to the *Privacy Act 1988* (Cth).

Chapter 3

Scope: expansion of the framework and write access

Abstract

Chapter 3 focuses on the key challenges associated with defining the scope of *CDS 3.0* frameworks: their sectoral coverage, the integration of action initiation and cross-border connectivity. *Section 3.1* discusses the practical challenges of enabling an economy-wide *CDS 3.0* regime spanning multiple sectors. This is important since third-generation *CDS* frameworks are unlikely to be launched across all sectors of the economy at once. Considering the experience of Australia's cross-sectoral Consumer Data Right, this section discusses how *CDS 3.0* regimes could be strategically expanded from a handful of preselected sectors to the rest of the economy – either via sectoral designations, or by means of a principle of reciprocity. *Section 3.2* proceeds with a discussion about the relevance of 'action initiation' (or 'write access') functionality, which allows customers to permit service providers to act upon the information shared through a third-generation *CDS* framework (e.g., by initiating payments and changing their product or service provider). *Section 3.3* concludes with an analysis of the desirability, potential and risks of cross-border connectivity among domestic *CDS 3.0* systems.

3.1 Economy-wide expansion

As explained in Section 1.6, isolating customer data within public and private sector enterprises impedes the development of innovative data-powered products and services, undermines competition and, importantly, deprives customers of the ability to control and use their data. As the 'lifeblood of economic development,' customer data should flow freely in any given sector, to allow customers to capitalise on the full range of opportunities provided by their data. Customer data should also be able to move without restrictions across sectors, as information from one sector influences decision-making in other sectors.[1] Because the value of customer data resides in the uses to which it can be put,[2] extending customer data sharing to multiple sectors *increases the value of customer data by capitalising on synergies across sectors.*[3] This 'value creation' under existing *CDS 2.0* frameworks remains limited.

The PSD2 and the UK open banking framework, for example, were created to ensure more competitive, transparent and secure *payment* processes.

DOI: 10.4324/9781003414216-3

However, these regimes are limited, as they do not encompass various financial products and services like mortgages and savings accounts. In Australia, in contrast, the scope of open banking is considerably broader and mandates access to 29 different bank accounts (including savings, home loan, mortgage and personal loan accounts and business financing accounts).[4] Home loan applications vividly illustrate the advantages of the Australian approach.

Research data shows that customers often hesitate to switch providers even when staying with the current provider results in 'loyalty penalties.' Many UK customers pay higher mortgage rates due to the real or perceived inconvenience of switching or lack of awareness of superior alternatives.[5] Likewise, in Australia, while home loans as a product offer the greatest potential for savings, they remain the most difficult to switch.[6] Customers with a variable rate home loan over four years old typically pay $1,000 more each year in interest than they need to pay for every $250,000 outstanding on their loan.[7] By allowing data sharing from a broader set of bank accounts, the Australian open banking system helps customers secure these potential savings by streamlining and expediting the process of transitioning to a superior home loan.

Where customer data sharing is expanded to other economy sectors, the benefits are multiplied. While banking data is indispensable for financial planning and loan assessment purposes, combining that data with superannuation and insurance data and information on energy or telecommunications usage produces a much richer picture of the customer's financial situation – it allows the provider to better measure, and more accurately price, risk and thus shape new and better credit offers. In other words, *combining data sets results in an outcome that is greater than the sum of the parts.*

For a range of reasons – be it funding, the lack of a precedent to learn from or the unlikely simultaneous availability of the requisite cross-sectoral expertise – it is highly improbable that *CDS 3.0* frameworks will be launched across all sectors of the economy at once. Rather, in any given jurisdiction (as has been the case so far), data sharing will most likely be sequential: first launched in individual sectors (such as banking) and then gradually expanded to other economy sectors.

Still, the practical challenges of building a gradual, cross-sectoral or even economy-wide customer data sharing ecosystem are many and diverse.

To begin with, *balancing system maturity with expansion* is no straightforward task. In pursuit of benefits flowing from the *CDS 3.0* systems, regulators in jurisdictions with prescriptive customer data sharing approaches (see Section 2.1) may choose to push for a pace of adoption that industries may struggle with. Certainly, moving at a pace of a slower participant may lead to the *CDS 3.0* system's stagnation; yet, advancing at a pace that most participants struggle to maintain equally risks failure.[8] Sector maturity may therefore serve as an indicator of a *CDS* regime's readiness to move forward. Indeed, the advantage of a gradual, 'one sector at a time' approach is that it helps to ensure that customer data sharing in a given sector functions as intended. In consultations on the Statutory Review of the CDR in Australia, for example, numerous stakeholders emphasised that 'without fully completing one sector first, the rollout would not benefit from lessons learnt and could repeat the same mistakes in relation to new sectors.'[9]

Aspirations for a rapid expansion of customer data sharing across economy sectors may also conflict with the need to ensure appropriate range and depth of functionalities within *CDS 3.0*. As will be shown in Section 3.2, some *CDS 2.0* frameworks (such as the UK's open banking regime) – while significantly narrower in their reach – allow for important functionalities (specifically, 'action initiation') that the CDR is yet to implement. The consultative process on the Statutory Review of the CDR revealed a considerable tension between the Australian government's vision of a digital economy enhanced by a widespread implementation of the CDR and the desire to deepen and refine the CDR's functionality in already designated sectors.[10]

Identifying the (next) most suitable sector(s) for the establishment of or inclusion in a *CDS 3.0* ecosystem may be easier said than done. As we show in Section 3.2, some sectors (such as energy and telecommunications) may offer better use cases and thus a higher customer uptake that would spur ecosystem growth; yet, other considerations and historical factors (such as the availability of an overseas precedent to learn from) may lead a *CDS 3.0* journey of a given jurisdiction in a different direction. In Australia, for instance, the decision to prioritise banking over other sectors of economy was grounded, amongst other considerations, on the strong foundation established by the obligations that a bank holds towards its customers. As explained by the chair of the review into open banking in Australia, Scott Farrell:

> A bank has a duty to keep a customer's money safe and to pay it to others at the customer's direction. Similarly, a bank has a duty to keep its customer's information confidential. An obligation for a bank to provide the customer's information to others at the customer's direction makes sense – both money and information are valuable and the bank would not have either without the customer. In this way, the long-established banker-customer relationship can help guide Open Banking's construction and once the framework is built, it can be extended to other sectors.[11]

Certain economy sectors could benefit more readily from reductions of data-related barriers. Concentration and market prices usually provide major indicators for the sectors to which customer data sharing arrangements could be extended most immediately.[12] Indeed, across jurisdictions, notable market concentration and resulting elevated prices served as a major driver for regulating or promoting customer data sharing in the banking sector. For instance, in Australia, it has been found that the consistently high profits of the top four banks – Commonwealth Bank, ANZ, NAB and Westpac – were attributed more to market conditions that frequently disadvantaged their competitors than to exceptional performance.[13] The same rationale has driven the Australian government to designate energy and telecommunications as priority sectors to which the CDR should apply following banking.[14]

The level of digital maturity of a given sector may also have a bearing on its relative prioritisation in the overall customer data sharing expansion scheme. Sectors with more sophisticated digital infrastructure and greater levels of data standardisation are certainly easier to integrate in a *CDS 3.0* regime.[15] Customer behavioural insights (such as irrational loyalty to providers who make customers pay loyalty penalties) could serve as another point of guidance on which sector may benefit from the inclusion in a *CDS 3.0* regime.

Finding the most appropriate *method* of consistently expanding customer data sharing across economy sectors could be yet another challenge, particularly in light of the resistance to the roll-out coming from the established data holders, such as banks or major utilities companies.[16] For *CDS 3.0* systems to be effective, prioritisation and sequencing of the sector roll-out should proceed with due consideration of how the overarching (and potentially conflicting) objectives of such systems could be best realised (see Sections 1.6 and 2.2). One of the underlying benefits of an 'umbrella structure' as adopted in Australia, is that the goals that the CDR aims to fulfil continue to be reflected in sectoral regulation while sector-specific needs are equally accommodated. Moreover, compared to an approach where *CDS 3.0* may be implemented through distinct sector-specific legal frameworks such an 'umbrella structure' may facilitate better coordination between regulators overseeing the implementation of a *CDS 3.0* regime.

As shown in Section 1.5, the CDR is grounded on the statutory framework of the *Treasury Laws (Consumer Data Right) Act 2019* (Cth) (*CDR Act*)[17] with four core components, of which the following are most relevant. The first is the enabling legislation, the *CDR Act*, which introduces Part IVD into the *CCA*.[18] The *CDR Act* outlines the underlying objectives of the CDR and sets out the regime's foundational elements, including the role and functions of the regulatory bodies charged with establishing and enforcing the regime's rules, accreditation requirements and minimum privacy protections.[19] CDR Designation Instruments issued under Part IVD of the *CDR Act* constitute the second component of the regime: they designate sectors of the Australian economy for the purposes of the CDR.[20] Sector designations play an important role in identifying parameters for customer data sharing within the sector: they specify the classes of data subject to the CDR and the class(es) of persons who hold the designated information (the data holders). Importantly, the requirement to disclose certain data and the circumstances in which data sharing is required are laid out in the third component of the framework – the *CDR Rules*[21] which, to the extent feasible, have been formulated to be universally applicable across economy sectors. Sector-specific provisions are set out in sector-specific schedules, to be revised over time as the CDR framework evolves.

The instrument of sectoral designation thus facilitates the CDR's gradual expansion, while the *CDR Rules* and schedules ensure consistency, comprehensibility and predictability of data sharing requirements across the economy, while avoiding the regulatory duplication that most likely would be unavoidable were each economy sector governed by a distinct legislative or regulatory instrument.

Further, depending on the jurisdiction and the pace of its *CDS 3.0* roll-out, *increasing or sustaining the efficiency of expanding cross-sectoral customer data sharing regimes* could present yet another challenge.

In jurisdictions with facilitative or market-driven approaches to customer data sharing (see Section 2.1), mandating customer data sharing may accelerate the adoption of *CDS 3.0*, provided that regulatory burden and costs of compliance are manageable for participants, particularly new market entrants. Still, since it is customers who generate data and the customer consent that triggers customer data sharing, sufficient take-up rate among customers is crucial to secure efficient operationalisation of *CDS 3.0*. Customer education campaigns may be necessary to ensure that customers understand the benefits and perils of *CDS 3.0* regimes and feel confident and, above all, keen to participate.[22]

Therefore, centring the unfolding of a *CDS 3.0* system around *use cases* that offer the most value for customers could meaningfully facilitate cross-sector and economy-wide customer data sharing.[23] For example, the CDR's all-encompassing approach for banking data sets has been criticised by some industry stakeholders as effectively prioritising quantity over quality. By including a range of products used by mainly sophisticated institutional customers (as noted in Section 2.2.2, CDR's scope is not limited to individual customers) the argument is that the CDR does not pay adequate attention to the needs and interests of ordinary, individual customers.[24] Subsequently, a whole of economy strategic assessment conducted in Australia in 2021 found that 'a data purpose-driven approach,' which considers how future data sets could enhance already designated data sets to deliver the most engaging customer use cases, offered the most promising route for a more agile and focused expansion of the CDR.[25] Open finance – with the concurrent evaluation and designation of data sets across the merchant acquiring, non-bank lending, superannuation and general insurance sectors – was identified as a domain which allows prioritisation of a smaller mix of data sets promising to unlock a broader array of more valuable use cases and better customer outcomes.[26] As illustrated in the assessment: 'combining a few key datasets in superannuation and general insurance would support applications that provide consumers with a richer picture of their current and expected financial circumstances and will support improved financial planning, and key life decisions such as asset purchases, preparing for retirement or change in employment circumstances while balancing implementation considerations.'[27]

Notably, economies with an established customer digital identity system (such as Aadhaar in India) enjoy a significant advantage in relation to horizontal data integration and sharing that Australia currently does not enjoy. Bringing together customer data sets from across sectors and providers under the CDR is complicated by the reliance on different sector-specific unique customer identifiers: an address and/or metering device used by energy providers, a customer identification number used in banking, a tax file number for the identification of individuals used by the Australian Taxation Office, and so on.[28] Against this background, the Statutory Review of the CDR found that to support future cross-sectoral use cases 'an overarching unique identifying layer or data interoperability mechanism between unique identifiers within the CDR [is needed] to reliably identify the consumer and manage consents while maintaining appropriate privacy protections.'[29]

Reciprocity could also stimulate cross-sectoral and economy-wide expansion of customer data sharing. This mechanism ensures that, in response to a customer request, data recipients provide customer data they already hold to other data recipients to the extent that such data is 'equivalent' to the data they have received. Reciprocity enables a system in which 'all eligible entities participate fully – both as data holders and data recipients' and – through the concept of 'equivalent data' – increases the scope of data available for customers.[30]

Currently, the CDR's approach to reciprocity remains constrained in that reciprocity arrangements are allowed only in relation to data laid out in the sectoral designation, meaning that types of data that are notably different from those already encompassed by the CDR cannot become subject to the CDR regime under reciprocity, until a sectoral assessment and an official designation of the sector by the minister has taken place.[31] To illustrate, a data-powered service provider that receives banking data under the CDR yet holds no data equivalent to banking data has no obligation to share any customer data it may have. This outcome is hardly satisfactory. Indeed, if a data recipient can offer its customer a better deal because of combining the information it already has on this customer with the data accessed via the CDR, then most likely that customer's current provider could equally generate a better offering if the information held by the data recipient was available to that provider.[32] Against this background and to encourage competitive neutrality and fairness as data sharing is expanded across economy, the Inquiry into the Future Directions of the CDR recommended that reciprocal obligations of an accredited data recipient should not be limited by the sectoral designation of that data recipient but should apply even where they hold equivalent data on sectors which are not designated.[33] The criteria for what constitutes 'equivalent' data should be clearly defined, however, to ensure transparency in implementation.[34]

Still, certain substantial risks remain. Compliance costs, which may particularly affect smaller data recipients who will have to set up and maintain infrastructure for both the supply and receipt of data, may incentivise those data recipients to bypass the *CDS 3.0* regime in favour of other data access methods.[35] At the same time, established data holders (who are often also data recipients) profit from a greater opportunity to capture additional market share.[36] To lessen the potential for reciprocity obligations to deter new entrants from the *CDS 3.0* regimes, it may be prudent to include temporary exemptions for smaller data recipients.[37]

3.2   Action initiation

A significant, if not *the most* significant, factor in the adoption and expansion of *CDS 3.0* regimes is the functionality of 'action initiation' (also known as 'write access') which allows customers to permit a service provider to initiate actions on their behalf (e.g., initiate payments).[38] Without action initiation a *CDS 3.0* regime remains underdeveloped, mostly functioning as a comparison website.[39]

In contrast, where action initiation is enabled, a much broader array of functions and thus a greater range of products and services are available to customers. For example, changing providers becomes a much easier and faster process – potentially a matter of a couple of clicks on a mobile device or a computer.[40] This point is effectively demonstrated by telecommunications and energy. Customers pay too much for their mobile phone and electricity usage. Even where service providers contact customers to offer a better payment plan, the latter are often too busy to respond and even if they did, mostly rightly assume that comparing different offers will be onerous and better postponed. With action initiation offering a seamless customer experience in switching service providers, there will be no need to take unsolicited phone calls to swap providers. Crucially, the existing provider will not have the chance to retain a customer by presenting a more appealing offer when they make contact to terminate their contract. The provider will only learn about the loss of customers post factum, at least in sectors where provider change is straightforward. For this reason, one may well argue that energy and telecommunications offer a better starting point for a *CDS 3.0* regime than banking, since transferring one's mobile phone or energy account is much easier than switching banks.

Thus, as indicated in Section 1.6, action initiation is well positioned to gradually eliminate loyalty penalties and restore a commercial morality, a fundamental fairness, that modern businesses often ignore.[41] Some decades ago, it was a common belief among businesses that all customers should be offered the same price. In Australia, for example, prior to 1995, price discrimination by businesses was prohibited under Section 49 of the *Trade Practices Act 1974* (Cth). Specifically, it was unlawful to 'discriminate between purchasers of goods of like grade and quality in relation to,' inter alia, price. Today, however, customer loyalty is often exploited (as illustrated in Section 3.1, many customers who have maintained home loans for an extended period find themselves paying significantly elevated interest rates compared to borrowers who have recently acquired home loans). By facilitating smoother transitions between products and services, cross-sectoral and economy-wide customer data sharing pushes providers to ensure fair treatment for all customers from the start, or face the risk of losing them to competitors.

While some elements of action initiation – namely 'payment initiation' – have been part of open banking in Europe and the UK from the inception of both regimes,[42] its implementation in Australia has been purposefully delayed. The government strongly believed that, for the CDR to thrive, it is essential for customers to first gain confidence that their data is handled securely and solely for the purposes they have authorised. Allowing third parties to act on customers' behalf from the start was regarded premature and likely to jeopardise the acceptance of the framework.[43]

In December 2021, however, responding to the *Final Report of the Inquiry into Future Directions for the Consumer Data Right*, the government announced it would amend the CDR regime to include action initiation in banking by enabling third party 'payment initiation' along with 'general action initiation,' including the options of switching between products and services, opening or closing accounts, automating the processes for undertaking loan, mortgage and other applications for products and services or 'one stop shop' budgeting applications.[44] The bill proposing to extend the CDR framework to include action initiation was finally introduced into Parliament in November 2022.[45] In May 2023, the Senate Economics Legislation Committee presented its report on the bill and recommended that the bill be passed.[46] In its 2023 Federal Budget, the government allocated $AUD 88.8 million over two years to further investment in the CDR with the focus on – among other things – undertaking detailed policy and design work on action and payment initiation.[47]

The wide range of use cases and benefits flowing from action initiation is contingent on how a *CDS 3.0* framework is designed, in particular the economy sectors within a *CDS 3.0* which will have the action initiation functionality enabled.[48] In Australia, the consultative process on action initiation identified a number of important considerations to guide the establishment of the action initiation framework under the CDR. These issues are unlikely to be uniquely Australian and may inform decision-making on the introduction of action initiation in other jurisdictions. We therefore now turn to these considerations. Specifically, we discuss potential regulatory hurdles that may need to be overcome to implement action initiation, digital readiness of relevant economy sectors, and the scope and risks of action initiation.

To begin with, certain sector-specific requirements, unless amended, may stand in the way of implementing action initiation. Account switching in some sectors, for example, may only be permitted where customers have consented in writing (as opposed to by electronic means). For action initiation to serve its purpose such friction points will need to be addressed by regulatory arrangements. Still, in some cases it may prove sensible to retain existing regulations and consider regulatory adjustments to the scope of action initiation. The consultative process on action initiation under the CDR concluded, for example, that the formal requirements to effect transfers of real and personal property security interests when transitioning from one secured lending product to another, while an obstacle to a seamless switching, should be retained.[49]

Compared to the (limited) functionality of customer data sharing, action initiation represents an added step in the interaction between *CDS 3.0* participants. Because of the range and complexity of actions that may be taken as a result of analysis of customer data, successful implementation of the action initiation functionality is likely to require a higher level of digital maturity of relevant economy sectors.[50] For action initiation to operate effectively, sectoral digital infrastructure would need to be such as to enable regime participants to seamlessly engage, authenticate and transact with customers exclusively online (as opposed to, for example, requiring a customer to phone to initiate an action). Still, the risks of market concentration and the ensuing reduction in competition remain even in digitally advanced sectors due to the costs associated with the implementation of action initiation functionality (see also Section 2.1). Market participants with a higher degree of digital preparedness and greater financial capacity to execute digital innovation may be able to take fuller advantage of action initiation faster and with less stress.[51] To mitigate these concerns and maintain a balanced market landscape, action initiation frameworks may need to consider additional regulatory, financial and other support measures for smaller service providers to ensure that the objective of improved competition can indeed be realised.

While designed to offer customers increased convenience and ease of engagement with the regime, the concept of action initiation has its limits. To minimise potential risks for customers (see further in this section) and ensure that service providers can successfully integrate this capability in their operational processes, the type of action that a customer is permitted to initiate is constrained to the types of action that data holders would ordinarily perform in the course of their business.[52] This is designed to protect data holders from being forced to perform actions they would not ordinarily perform.[53] Other limits may arise because[54] consultations with industry and consumer protection bodies could assist in identifying circumstances and actions that should remain beyond the scope of action initiation.

The sheer variety of actions that action initiation may facilitate increases the surface area for risks to customers. In contrast to data sharing proper, where the focus of customer protections is primarily on the privacy and confidentiality of the customer's data, the risks associated with action initiation are more diverse.[55] The functionality may be deliberately exploited for commercial gains, for example, where service providers repeatedly switch the customer's energy supplier to gain commissions or push to switch the customer's insurance provider by misrepresenting that the switch would be advantageous for the customer.[56] Australian legislators therefore emphasised that 'right penalties' that actively discourage the misuse of action initiation will be integral to the successful operation of the regime.[57] Apart from increased privacy and information security risks resulting, for example, from the additional data flows between the participants involved in initiating and performing the action,[58] action initiation may bring greater financial risks to customers (particularly in cases of wrongly initiated payments or accounts mistakenly opened on behalf of the customer). Without proper protections, action initiation could potentially allow a service provider to act against a customer's express preferences or interests.

A clear governance and responsibility framework is required to ensure these risks are appropriately managed. Thus, service providers seeking to initiate actions on customers' behalf will require accreditation (and additional conditions for accreditation may need to be imposed for the ability to initiate actions with greater potential for harm to customers).[59] As with data sharing proper, customer consent remains critical for triggering the functionality of action initiation. Finally, the allocation of liability between participants and provision of redress mechanisms for customers would also need to be factored into the design of the action initiation functionality.[60]

3.3 Cross-border connectivity

Given that states today are part of the 'larger global digital economy,'[61] we explore how domestic *CDS 3.0* systems might 'connect' with each other, the desirability of such connections and the challenges that may arise en route to what may one day be called '*CDS 4.0*' – an ecosystem of rules and practices allowing customers to direct their data to service providers residing *abroad* so these can offer customers a better value for money service *at home*. Likewise, customers could direct *overseas data holders* to share their data with service providers either at home or overseas (e.g., a PFM service for someone with bank accounts in several jurisdictions). Despite the differences in how *CDS 2.0* and *CDS 3.0* regimes have so far been implemented worldwide, the scope for interoperability is likely to attract increased attention in the future.[62] While some existing *CDS* frameworks already partially regulate cross-border disclosure of customer data,[63] further steps in that direction can certainly be expected in time from policymakers.

As illustrated in Section 1.6, *CDS 2.0* and *CDS 3.0* regimes share objectives to increase competition, promote innovation and serve and protect customers. The benefits of attaining these goals will be significantly amplified when the goals are international in scale. Connected national *CDS 3.0* frameworks could strongly foster competition and innovation. They could improve 'overall systemic competitiveness,' including *domestic sectoral competitiveness* but also *global competitiveness* of domestic service provid-ers.[64] Customers could benefit from a global pool of products and services (including investment and lending opportunities, better retail products, etc.). Crucially, given the enhanced privacy and information security controls of *CDS 3.0* systems, services will have the same or higher customer protection safeguards as exist under the domestic *CDS 3.0* regimes. Indeed, while the Future Directions Report and the Statutory Review of the CDR anticipated significant benefits for customers from cross-border data sharing,[65] research shows that data regulations that limit domestic and international data transfers might notably decrease productivity and economic outcomes.[66]

The fundamental question is: how can cross-border customer data sharing be enabled in principle and what is (or not) portable across borders?

As with domestic frameworks where data sharing is facilitated through rules, business protocols, practices flowing from those rules and technical standards,[67] customer data sharing across borders could be governed through bilateral or multilateral agreements (such as on the harmonisation of licensing and accreditation requirements for service providers) and technical standards.

In fact, some legislative and regulatory requirements on customer data sharing already apply across borders by definition as is the case with PSD2 in Europe (see Sections 1.6 and 3.1). Some existing *CDS 2.0* and *CDS 3.0* frameworks actively influence emerging regimes abroad: the UK prides itself on exporting open banking to around 80 other jurisdictions and New Zealand is developing a *CDS* system which closely resembles the Australian CDR.[68] Once the idea of cross-border *CDS* gains traction, we can expect greater regulatory alignment between participating states. For example, the Future Directions Report concluded that Australia 'should streamline accreditation to recognise foreign regimes where appropriate and seek mutual recognition with the United Kingdom.'[69] Importantly, 'regulatory alignment' does not suggest 'regulatory uniformity.' Rather, it recognises differences in regulatory frameworks and works towards 'bridges' necessary to enable service provid-ers to operate seamlessly across borders.[70] Still, some elements of the cross-border customer data sharing regime may prove harder to 'bridge': such as strict data localisation laws that heavily regulate personal data transfer across borders.[71] Furthermore, the more stringent the regulations governing the shar-ing of personal data in a jurisdiction, the more likely equivalent controls will be expected from the jurisdiction with which customer data is intended to be shared.

Another fundamental element of a cross-border *CDS* are technical stand-ards. Some key technical standards that operationalise *CDS* regimes are already in use in multiple *CDS 2.0* ecosystems.[72] To illustrate, a typical API ecosystem that involves customer data sharing relies on building blocks. These include (i) 'identity management' (protocols that define how identity informa-tion is transferred); (ii) 'data API specifications' (that describe what an API should be able to do and relevant data models) and (iii) an 'API security and authorisation framework' (which defines 'how parties are authenticated, how the authorisation and the data request and response are secured, how consent is captured and how message integrity is preserved'[73]). Analysis of some of the largest existing open banking regimes[74] reveals that the same identity protocol has been used by most (i.e., OpenID Connect 1.0); likewise, the majority of the studied regimes have adopted financial-grade API as their API security profile and rely on standardised consent flow and consent management APIs. Still, some technical elements of a *CDS* ecosystem may be jurisdiction specific. For example, most data API specifications remain proprietary with only a few applicable across borders, such as those of the Berlin Group (comprising ten European states) and Financial Data Exchange (comprising US and Canada).[75] Even then, experts assert that coexistence of multiple standards does not mean interoperability between those standards is unattainable.[76]

The risks of a *CDS 4.0* regime should be carefully considered. As discussed in Sections 1.6 and 5.2.2, despite stronger privacy and information security protocols, *CDS 3.0* systems substantially increase the number of entities that may access customer data (and thus the frequency of data transfers) with each additional entity potentially introducing a new point of vulnerability through which data could be compromised. These risks may be magnified, the more foreign service providers get access to customer data to 'outdo' domestic providers. Moreover, the dynamics of market concentration explained previously (Sections 2.1 and 3.2) are likely to resurface in a *CDS 4.0* system leading to some service providers establishing regional or even global monopoly on (certain) products and services.

Nonetheless, *CDS 4.0* regimes have the potential to evolve into vital connectors within the global economy provided governments work to harness their advantages effectively while mitigating associated risks.

Notes

1 European Commission, *A European Strategy for Data* (Communication from the Commission to the European Parliament, the Council, the European Economic and Social Committee and the Committee of the Regions, COM(2020) 66 final, 19 February 2020) 2 ('*A European Strategy for Data*').
2 Luciano Floridi, *Information: A Very Short Introduction* (Oxford University Press, 2010) 90; ACS, *Data Sharing Frameworks: Technical White Paper* (Report, September 2017) 21. See also *A European Strategy for Data* (n 1).
3 Australian Government, *Statutory Review of the Consumer Data Right* (Report, 2022) 42 ('*Statutory Review*').
4 *Competition and Consumer (Consumer Data Right) Rules 2020* (Cth) sch 3 cl 1.4 ('*CDR Rules*').
5 Chandana Asif et al., 'Financial Services Unchained: The Ongoing Rise of Open Financial Data', *McKinsey & Company* (Online, 11 July 2021) <www.mckinsey.com/industries/financial-services/our-insights/financial-services-unchained-the-ongoing-rise-of-open-financial-data>.
6 Treasury, Australian Government, *Inquiry into Future Directions for the Consumer Data Right* (Report, October 2020) 24 ('*Inquiry into Future Directions*').

7 Treasury, Australian Government, 'Implementation of an Economy-Wide Consumer Data Right' (Strategic Assessment Consultation Paper, 2021) 13.

8 *Statutory Review* (n 3) 42.

9 Ibid.

10 Ibid.

11 Treasury, Australian Government, *Review into Open Banking: Giving Customers Choice, Convenience and Confidence* (Report, December 2017) v ('*Review into Open Banking*').

12 Ross Buckley, Natalia Jevglevskaja and Scott Farrell, 'Australia's Data Sharing Regime: Six Lessons for Europe' (2022) 33(1) *King's Law Journal* 61, 81.

13 See Australian Competition and Consumer Commission, Submission No 17 to Productivity Commission, *Inquiry into Competition in the Australian Financial System* (September 2017) 8 <www.pc.gov.au/__data/assets/pdf_file/0019/221860/sub017-financial-system.pdf>.

14 Note, however, that the CDR's expansion to the telecommunications sector has been temporarily put on hold in mid-2023, to allow the regime to mature in finance and energy first. See Australian Government, 'Federal Budget' (26 May 2023) *Consumer Data Right Newsletter*.

15 'Implementation of an Economy-Wide Consumer Data Right' (n 7) 18.

16 Natalia Jevglevskaja and Ross Buckley, 'The Consumer Data Right: How to Realise This World-Leading Reform' (2022) 45(4) *UNSW Law Journal* 1589, 1619.

17 *Treasury Laws Amendment (Consumer Data Right) Act 2019* (Cth).

18 *Competition and Consumer Act 2010* (Cth) ('*CCA*').

19 Treasury, Australian Government, *Consumer Data Right Overview* (Booklet, September 2019) 9.

20 For instance, the *Consumer Data Right (Authorised Deposit-Taking Institutions) Designation 2019* (Cth) designated the banking sector.

21 *CDR Rules* (n 4).

22 Jevglevskaja and Buckley (n 16) 1620.

23 Treasury, Australian Government, *Strategic Assessment: Outcomes* (Report, January 2022) 7.

24 ABA, Submission to Treasury, *Statutory Review of the Consumer Data Right* (20 May 2022) 2 <https://treasury.gov.au/sites/default/files/2022-09/c2022-314513-australian_banking_association.pdf>.

25 *Strategic Assessment: Outcomes* (n 23) 6–8.

26 Ibid 8.

27 Ibid.

28 *Statutory Review* (n 3) 58–9.

29 Ibid 59.

30 See *Review into Open Banking* (n 11) 44; *Inquiry into Future Directions* (n 6) 215. See also Brad Carr, Daniel Pujazon and Pablo Urbiola, 'Reciprocity in Customer Data Sharing Frameworks' (Research Paper, Institute of International Finance, July 2018).

31 *CCA* (n 18) s 56AJ. See also *Inquiry into Future Directions* (n 6) 114.

32 *Inquiry into Future Directions* (n 6) 116.

33 Ibid recommendation 6.9. See also ABA (n 24) 7.

34 See also *Inquiry into Future Directions* (n 6) recommendation 6.10.

35 See *Statutory Review* (n 3) 51.

36 See, e.g., EY, 'Does the Existing Statutory Framework Support the Evolution of the Consumer Data Right?' (Response, May 2022); Basiq, *Statutory Review of the Consumer Data Right: Issues Paper* (Submission, 10 June 2022) <https://treasury.gov.au/sites/default/files/2022-09/c2022-314513-basiq.pdf>.

37 *Inquiry into Future Directions* (n 6) 117.

38 Explanatory Memorandum, Treasury Laws Amendment (Consumer Data Right) Bill 2022 (Cth) [1.2]–[1.3] ('Treasury Laws Memorandum').

39 'Comparison websites' are 'sites that generally compare products across a product category offered by a range of suppliers, according to specific characteristics provided by the consumer': *Inquiry into Future Directions* (n 6) 215.

40 Jevglevskaja and Buckley (n 16) 1607.

41 See also Productivity Commission, Australian Government, *Competition in the Australian Financial System* (Inquiry Report No 89, 29 June 2018) 13.

42 *Directive (EU) 2015/2366 of the European Parliament and of the Council of 25 November 2015 on Payment Services in the Internal Market, Amending Directives 2002/65/EC, 2009/110/EC and 2013/36/EU and Regulation (EU) No 1093/2010, and Repealing Directive 2007/64/EC* [2015] OJ L 337/35, art 4(15). In the UK, action initiation applies to transaction accounts only and to just nine banks: Deloitte, *Open Banking: Payment Initiation – Completing the Vision* (Open Banking Series, December 2019) 2 <www.deloitte.com/content/dam/assets-zone1/au/en/docs/industries/financial-services/2023/fsi-open-banking-december-2019.pdf. html?icid=learn_more_content_click>.

43 *Review into Open Banking* (n 11) 109.

44 Treasury, Australian Government, 'Government Response to the *Inquiry into Future Directions for the Consumer Data Right*' (Government Response, December 2021) 2. See also Explanatory Memorandum, Treasury Laws Amendment (Consumer Data Right) Bill 2022 (Cth) [1.8].

45 Treasury Laws Amendment (Consumer Data Right) Bill 2022. See 'Treasury Laws Amendment (Consumer Data Right) Bill 2022', *Parliament of Australia* (Web Page) <www.aph.gov.au/Parliamentary_Business/Bills_Legislation/Bills_Search_Results/Result?bId=r6950>.

46 Australian Government, 'Treasury Laws Amendment (Consumer Data Right) Bill 2022' (26 May 2023) *Consumer Data Right Newsletter*.

47 Australian Government, 'Budget 2023–24: Budget Strategy and Outlook' (Budget Paper No 1, 9 May 2023) 31. See also 'Federal Budget' (n 14).

48 *Inquiry into Future Directions* (n 6) 20.

49 Ibid 31.

50 Ibid 39.

51 Ibid. See also Damir Ćuća, 'Action Initiation: The Double-Edged Sword of Australia's Consumer Data Right', *Basiq* (Blog Post, 14 April 2023) <www.basiq.io/blog/action-initiation-the-double-edged-sword-of-australias-consumer-data-right/>.

52 Treasury Laws Memorandum (n 38) [1.11].

53 Ibid.

54 *Inquiry into Future Directions* (n 6) 48.

55 Financial Rights Legal Centre, Submission to Treasury, *Statutory Review of the Consumer Data Right* (12 May 2022) <https://financialrights.org.au/wp-content/uploads/2022/05/220421_CDRIndependentStatRev_FINAL.pdf>; Ibid 155.

56 Treasury Laws Memorandum (n 38) [1.89]–[1.91].

57 Ibid [101].

58 KPMG, *Privacy Impact Assessment on the Introduction of Action Initiation in the Consumer Data Right* (Report, September 2022) 7 [1.4.7].

59 *Inquiry into Future Directions* (n 6) 50.

60 Ibid 35.

61 *Statutory Review* (n 3) 59.

62 *Inquiry into Future Directions* (n 6) 200.

63 For example, disclosure of CDR data may occur to data recipients located outside Australia as long as these recipients are accredited under the CDR, see *CCA* (n 18) s 56EK(1)(c). For other cases where such disclosure is allowed, see *CCA* (n 18) ss

56(1)(d)–(f). In the EU, Chapter 5 of the *GDPR* regulates conditions under which transfer of data to jurisdictions outside the EU is permitted.

64 Deloitte, *The Ecosystem Imperative: Digital Transformation of Financial Services and Moving from Open Banking to Open Data* (Report, 2023) 20.

65 *Inquiry into Future Directions* (n 6) 14; *Statutory Review* (n 3) finding 3.3.

66 World Economic Forum, *Data Free Flow with Trust (DFFT): Paths Towards Free and Trusted Data Flows* (Report, May 2020) 9. See also Martina Francesca Ferracane, Janez Kren and Erik van der Marel, 'Do Data Policy Restrictions Impact the Productivity Performance of Firms and Industries?' (DTE Working Paper No 1, 2018).

67 OpenID, *Open Banking and Open Data: Ready to Cross Borders?* (Report, January 2023) 10.

68 See 'What the Future Holds for Open Banking', *Open Banking* (Web Page, 3 November 2022) <www.openbanking.org.uk/news/what-the-future-holds-for-open-banking/>.

69 *Inquiry into Future Directions* (n 6) xii.

70 See also ibid 200.

71 For a detailed analysis, see W Gregory Voss, 'Cross-Border Data Flows, the GDPR, and Data Governance' (2020) 29(3) *Washington International Law Journal* 485.

72 OpenID (n 67) 12.

73 Ibid 12.

74 UK, US, Australia, Brazil, EU and India.

75 OpenID (n 67) 17.

76 Ibid 7.

Chapter 4

Service providers' perspective: the quest for greater participation

Abstract

This chapter views *CDS 3.0* from the perspective of a key group of stakeholders – service providers which facilitate the sharing of customer data. *Section 4.1* addresses the challenge of designing a balanced accreditation framework for recipients of customer data which allows sufficient participation without compromising on security. *Section 4.2* explores whether and how unaccredited persons may be granted access to customer data in a *CDS 3.0* ecosystem, while *Section 4.3* investigates why service providers might choose to rely on alternative data sharing practices (such as screen-scraping) despite the perceived benefits of third-generation *CDS*. On the basis of Australia's Consumer Data Right framework, *Section 4.4* evaluates the practice of protecting the interests of service providers through regulatory 'safe harbours' (which grant immunity to legal proceedings if certain formal criteria are satisfied). Lastly, *Section 4.5* explores the incentives for data holders to maintain the quality and usability of customer data shared with potential competitors through the *CDS 3.0* ecosystem.

4.1 Accreditation challenges

The success of *CDS 3.0* systems largely depends on customers having confidence that entities handling their data in those systems will do so safely. As will be illustrated in Section 5.2.1, in the eyes of customers, accreditation demonstrates the service providers' capability and willingness to faithfully follow the rules and standards of *CDS 3.0* frameworks.

From the perspective of service providers, accreditation is primarily an 'entry ticket' to the customer data sharing environment – a ticket that attests to their operational and financial fitness and credibility. Major jurisdictions with mandated second-generation *CDS* frameworks impose some kind of licensing or authorisation requirements. The EU's PSD2, for example, specifies a range of conditions a payment initiation service provider should meet for its application for the authorisation to be successful, such as: the 'governance arrangements and internal control mechanisms'[1]; a 'process in place to file, monitor, handle and follow up a security incident'[2]; and a 'process in place to file, monitor, track and restrict access to sensitive payment data.'[3] The

DOI: 10.4324/9781003414216-4

UK adopted a system of 'whitelisting' (accreditation) of approved parties by 'competent authorities' which translates the requirements of PSD2 into UK legislation.[4] Only whitelisted parties are given access to customer data under the UK's open banking regime. Likewise, in Australia, to have CDR data disclosed to them, service providers must be accredited (for exceptions, see below in this section and Section 4.2). A range of criteria must be satisfied: an accredited data recipient must (i) be a fit and proper person or organisation[5]; (ii) have processes in place to adequately protect data[6]; (iii) have internal dispute resolution processes[7]; (iv) belong to a relevant external dispute resolution scheme[8]; (v) hold adequate insurance for 'the risk of CDR consumers not being properly compensated for any loss that might reasonably be expected to arise from a breach of obligations' under the CDR framework[9] and (vi) have an Australian address for service.[10]

By requiring all applicants to meet the same minimum obligations for handling and protecting customer data,[11] accreditation requirements create a level-playing field among participating businesses and serve as a consumer protection tool (see also Section 2.2.2).[12] Accredited entities must comply with ongoing obligations to maintain their accreditation. Non-compliance may result in suspension or revocation of the accreditation.[13]

Designing an appropriate accreditation framework is not without challenges, however, the foremost being the need to strike the right balance between the requirements for accreditation and security of (customer) data sharing. Certainly, customers need assurance that the service providers participating in the system can handle their data safely and securely. However, requirements that are overly stringent or burdensome, impose prohibitive costs or require unrealistic investment of time, are more likely to erect barriers to entry than facilitate meaningful inclusion of service providers.[14] To illustrate, the inaugural accreditation model in Australia which included only one – unrestricted – level of accreditation came under heavy critique for unfairly benefitting large incumbent financial institutions.[15] Above all, accreditation costs have been argued to be prohibitively high for smaller market players, such as non-banks, and the process of accreditation was found by some to be excessively challenging and too lengthy.[16] As a result, the Australian government introduced 'tiered' accreditation. In addition to the highest (unrestricted) level of accreditation, another level – that is, 'sponsored accreditation' – was added which is easier to attain but also imposes certain limitations on participation in the CDR system of the 'sponsored' participant.[17] Besides, access to the CDR has been expanded through 'the representative model' and to 'trusted advisers,' neither of which require accreditation (see also Section 4.2).[18] Most recently, the circle of unaccredited entities that are allowed to receive customer data was broadened even further for a particular group of customers, that is, 'CDR business consumers' (see Section 4.2). And yet, despite ever more participants joining the system through alternative pathways, the criticisms have not subsided, with some still claiming the process remains too costly, too lengthy and too complex.[19] Moreover, some industry participants have lamented the incoherence of accreditation requirements under the CDR with those of some other government initiatives, such as requirements imposed on the Digital Service Providers under the Operational Security Framework for the Australian Taxation Office. They pointed to unreasonable demands on businesses requiring them to go through numerous accreditation processes for schemes centred around safeguarding data privacy and security.[20] These criticisms point to the need for further improvement of the CDR framework, and have been duly noted by government.[21]

Another important issue to consider is who should perform the accreditation role. The consultative process on the implementation of open banking in Australia identified two possible options: an industry-led accreditation utility or a regulatory agency. For reasons that an industry run utility may struggle to appropriately coordinate diverse views of aspiring CDR participants and to meaningfully balance privacy and efficiency considerations because of the potential bias towards incumbent institutions, the decision was taken in favour of the latter.[22] As a result, Australia's chief competition regulator – the ACCC – was designated to assess applicants' suitability for CDR participation and to manage the Register of Accredited Persons and Data Holders.[23]

4.2   Disclosure to non-accredited service providers

The competition promotion objective of *CDS 3.0* frameworks can only be achieved when new use cases for customer data developed by service providers offer better customer experience and more choice for customers, which is only achievable when the *CDS 3.0* ecosystem is widely used. As discussed in Section 4.1, the process of accreditation may present substantial challenges, despite the need for service providers wishing to 'plug into' the *CDS 3.0* ecosystem to be subject to strict regulatory controls. However, this raises the question: if accreditation proves cumbersome and expensive, should this requirement be waived for certain service providers and if so, which ones and on what grounds?

Australia's Consumer Data Right offers a useful example of an attempt to tackle this challenge. The original design of the CDR framework did not enable non-accredited persons to receive CDR data in any circumstances. This rule equally applied to different groups of professional advisers, who despite the lack of CDR accreditation were already subject to various professional requirements and standards. Faced with the choice to continue using the traditional channels for transmitting customer data (such as e-mail) or to become accredited and tap into the CDR ecosystem, some affected businesses challenged the authorisation requirements as disproportional. In particular, the business model of mortgage brokers, who operate as 'a small business or sole operator,' was cited as one of the reasons they are 'unlikely to be able to support the technology platforms and software services required to manage CDR data as specified in the CDR Rules.'[24]

Two alternative approaches were considered: (i) a light-touch mode of accreditation for professional advisers and (ii) a special non-accreditation pathway enabling certain regulated professionals to access CDR data. Interestingly, the business community was split regarding the best way forward.

4.2.1 Light-touch accreditation for professional advisers

Supporters of a separate accreditation tier came up with different eligibility criteria. Deloitte proposed three alternative options for defining the additional tiers: (i) '[t]iering based on the attributes of the CDR data being shared' (enabling lower tier recipients to access only basic customer information, such as account credit limits and opening/closing account balances), (ii) '[t]iering based on the sensitivity of the CDR data' (enabling higher tier recipients to access 'sensitive data attributes such as data from minors or, at a future point, health data') and (iii) '[t]iering based on standardised and/or approved uses of CDR data' (enabling lower tier recipients to receive CDR data for lower risk use cases, such as data aggregation).[25] The Financial Planning Association of Australia stressed the importance of accommodating professional advisers of different sizes and business models: 'Privacy and information security requirements should be designed in a manner that allows sole practitioners, not just large financial services firms, to become accredited.'[26]

In contrast, opponents of an extra accreditation tier, like Westpac, sought to prevent the potential dilution of customer protections, arguing that 'there should be *no lesser obligations in terms of security, privacy or consent.*'[27]

4.2.2 Non-authorisation pathway for professional advisers

The alternative, and more radical, proposal to grant certain professional advisers access to CDR data without any (even lower-tier) authorisation similarly attracted opposing views.

The Australian Privacy Foundation argued strongly against this approach noting that '[a]ny inclusion of *non-accredited parties* presents a *risk* for consumers using the system.'[28] This view was shared by the Financial Rights Legal Centre: 'All handlers of CDR data . . . *should be accredited.*'[29]

Overall, the opponents viewed the non-accreditation pathway as a 'backdoor' to valuable customer data that generated additional risks, particularly 'in the absence of economy-wide data protection reform.'[30]

Despite this opposition, an independent review on the future directions for the Consumer Data Right in Australia deemed *any* accreditation requirements for professional advisers excessive: 'Requiring entities, who are subject to existing regulations and accountable for the use of consumer's data under those regulations, to obtain *accreditation* (even at a lower tier) would be *disproportionate.*'[31]

4.2.3   Accreditation exemption for 'trusted advisers'

The debate concluded with the adoption of *Competition and Consumer (Consumer Data Right) Amendment Rules (No. 1) 2021* (2021 CDR Amendment Rules),[32] which enabled disclosure of CDR data to six types of professional service providers called 'trusted advisers' without CDR accreditation.[33] These categories include (i) qualified *accountants*; (ii) persons admitted to the *legal profession*; (iii) registered *tax agents, BAS agents* and *tax (financial) advisers*; (iv) *financial counselling agencies*; (v) 'relevant providers' within the meaning of the *Corporations Act 2001* (Cth); and (vi) mortgage brokers.[34]

Despite the apparent benefits for business users, 'trusted advisers' are effectively exempted from the application of the CDR framework and are not part of the CDR ecosystem. This outcome raises concerns for the other group of CDR users – customers, especially individual consumers. The corresponding implications are discussed in Section 5.2.

4.2.4   Accreditation exemption for representatives

The 2021 CDR Amendment Rules introduced another exemption from accreditation known as the 'representative model.' The latter enables an unaccredited service provider (the 'representative') to enter into a contract with an accredited person (the 'principal') whereby the representative uses the CDR data to provide services to the CDR consumer, while the principal requests CDR data for that purpose and discloses it to the representative.[35] Under this arrangement, the representative largely replaces the principal in its interactions with the customer:

> From the point of view of a CDR consumer who is the customer of a CDR representative, the consumer deals with the CDR representative, as if it were an accredited person, and may not deal with the principal at all. The consumer requests the goods or services from the CDR representative; the CDR representative identifies the CDR data that it needs in order to provide the goods and services; the consumer gives their consent to the CDR representative for the collection and use of the CDR data. The consumer is informed that the CDR principal will do the actual collecting, but as a background detail.[36]

Unlike 'trusted advisers' discussed in the previous subsection, CDR representatives are not excluded from the CDR framework. Despite being exempted from accreditation requirements, representatives are nonetheless subject to a range of obligations, many of which mirror those of their principal. In particular, a representative must comply with certain Privacy Safeguards and protect

CDR data in accordance with the *CDR Rules* 'as if it were the principal.'[37] On top of that, the principal 'must ensure that the CDR representative complies with its requirements under the arrangement'[38] – failure to do so is enforceable as a civil penalty provision.

4.2.5 Accreditation exemption for recipients of business customer data

The 2023 amendments of the *CDR Rules* introduced the new concept of 'CDR business consumer,' which covers CDR consumers that (i) are not individuals or (ii) have an active ABN.[39] Such businesses received preferential status enabling them to share CDR data with unaccredited entities that are not 'trusted advisers.'[40] Empowering 'CDR business consumers' is expected to boost participation in the CDR:

> Stakeholder feedback indicated that the previous CDR Rules did not cover the range of advisers or services typically used by businesses. This amendment provides a more comprehensive solution to support the participation of business consumers (particularly small businesses) and accounting platforms in the CDR.[41]

By enabling additional non-accredited persons to receive CDR data, these amendments have further exacerbated the boundary problem highlighted in Section 2.2. Indeed, the revised *CDR Rules* incorporate exemptions from accreditation that are based not only on the *types of recipients* of CDR data (with special provisions for trusted advisers and representatives) – but also on the *type of customer* in question: unlike most individuals, 'CDR business consumers' are allowed to choose the recipients of their data freely and regardless of accreditation (with the exception of one particular scenario).[42]

4.3 Alternative data sharing practices

As Section 1.6 shows, one of the underlying objectives of third-generation *CDS* frameworks is to make data sharing easier, more convenient and safer than other modes of sharing customer data available on the market.[43] Such alternative methods include, for example, credit reporting regimes, bilateral data sharing arrangements between entities offering financial services and the infamous practice of SS. In Australia, for example, credit providers have traditionally been required to furnish specific details regarding customer credit accounts to credit reporting agencies (e.g., Illion, Equifax and Experian).[44] Banks have frequently established one-on-one agreements with selected data-driven service providers (e.g., budgeting software companies) to share data so as to provide extra functionality to their clients.[45] Data aggregators and fintechs have long obtained data by means of SS technologies.[46]

SS is particularly disconcerting. As will be shown in Section 5.2.2, it represents an inherently unsafe online practice that significantly undermines not only customer protection safeguards but also progress of open banking and open finance (and by extension also of *CDS 3.0* systems). Nonetheless, the practice remains prevalent worldwide and needs to be reassessed – particularly by jurisdictions interested in establishing effective third-generation *CDS* ecosystems – or SS may never cease to exist.

As mentioned previously, SS involves customers sharing their online banking login credentials with third parties (e.g., service providers) who then 'scrape' customer data from the internet banking interfaces (without further identification vis-à-vis the account hosting institutions) to offer customers financial products and services (see Section 1.6). As of 2021, over 4 million Canadians – that is over 10% of the country's population – used financial services utilising SS.[47] According to the Financial Data Exchange,[48] as of 2020, data access and sharing for nearly one quarter of the US population – that is 65–85 million US consumers – was enabled via shared customer login credentials.[49] In Australia, too, SS has boomed. In 2001, only about 5,000 Australians a year were using it, whereas by 2017 over two million Australians were doing so – and numbers are likely to have increased since.[50]

Businesses have favoured SS as a data transfer technology primarily due to its convenience, efficiency and cost-effectiveness. Where no mandate to share data via structured data feeds – APIs – has been put in place, having customer account credentials means that a service provider does not need to negotiate access to customer data with the account-holding institution. Without customer account credentials, a business is left no choice but to negotiate data access via APIs which is a costly and time-consuming process. Where API connections are not available or the account-holding bank is unwilling to cooperate, customers are usually lost, since the service to them cannot be provided. However, even in the case of mandated and 'open' APIs – that are characterised by their (relatively) standardised format and accessibility to third parties at little to no cost – creating links to APIs, conducting testing and sustaining these connections demands a considerable investment of both financial resources and time.[51] It has been argued that establishing API connections can be even more daunting than developing the APIs themselves, especially when the objective is to establish connections with numerous financial institutions across various markets.[52]

In Europe, for example, three main API standards currently dominate the market – UK Open Banking Standard, Berlin Group's NextGenPSD2 XS2A Framework Standard and STET PSD2 API Framework – comprising regional requirements and further specifications, which can often be additionally customised by individual banks.[53] Whereas each data holder (i.e., bank) has, at most, one API to implement, fintechs providing account information and/ or payment initiation services[54] must implement numerous APIs, depending on the services they currently offer and their market reach.[55] The continuous monitoring of these API connections for potential downtime, upgrades and enhancements entails substantial effort, prompting many businesses to delegate these responsibilities to external service providers.

In contrast, the process for setting up technology to receive data via SS is fast, as it bypasses the data holder's systems and the required authorisation of data sharing.[56] Crucially, SS is argued to offer access to greater and more granular data. Held in a data collector's database, this data can be accessed at any time provided customer credentials remain unaltered or data access permission is not revoked.[57] Dedicated interfaces appear to pale in comparison, especially when banks decide to restrict the data accessible via APIs, decrease the connection speed or limit the availability of the APIs.[58]

Further grounds for defending SS include overly burdensome accreditation requirements – either real or perceived – under mandated data sharing regimes, like the CDR. As shown in Section 4.1, many of the Australian fintechs have argued that the CDR's accreditation regime erects barriers too steep for them to overcome effectively compelling them to use SS.[59] Some businesses even claim to pursue purely altruistic reasons, namely helping customers realise their autonomy, since customers have a choice to share their data via SS or via alternative techniques.[60] This 'choice,' however, is often a fiction, given that many customers may not realise that 'they have given their login details to someone other than their bank.'[61]

Most importantly, however, it is argued that SS must be retained to serve as a yardstick by which to evaluate the effectiveness of open banking and open finance initiatives. The Review into Open Banking in Australia, for instance, observed that '[s]hould those competing approaches [that is SS] become more actively used than those specified under Open Banking, this will provide a valuable signal to regulatory authorities that the design of Open Banking may need to be revisited.'[62] Moreover, some predict that SS will meaningfully complement open banking (and by extension, *CDS 3.0* systems) even past open banking's full implementation.[63] For example, SS may be necessary to complement data obtained via APIs in cases where the quantity and quality of the API-derived data are inadequate or subpar (for instance, SS may be employed to assist in cleaning and rectifying data segments and carrying out data reconciliation[64]), or to provide a redundancy fail-safe when the bank's dedicated interfaces are down or malfunction.[65]

So, what is one left to conclude? Certainly, SS holds historical significance. In the early days of the fintech industry, numerous businesses, confronted with the reluctance of established market players to share customer data, found themselves compelled to make a choice between resorting to SS or having no access to data. As one would anticipate, they opted for SS which has played a pivotal role in dismantling the barriers that banks had used as shields and has empowered fintechs to compete more effectively.[66] If fintech companies had relied on the banks to develop and publicly release their APIs, the fintech sector might not have come into existence, or it might have offered significantly fewer attractive products and services. Nonetheless, as we argue, SS should not come at the detriment of data security nor make it easier to exploit financially vulnerable customers (see Section 5.2.2). Most importantly, however, there is a genuine concern that accreditation costs under *CDS 3.0* regimes (as demonstrated by the case of the CDR in Australia, see Section 4.1), business inertia and path dependence could converge to prolong the use of SS, even when it is no longer advantageous for customers and the broader economy.

4.4 Safe harbours and legal certainty

Few considerations are as important for service providers as legal certainty and predictability of regulatory oversight and intervention – particularly with innovative and largely untested legal frameworks like *CDS 3.0*. Given the novelty of this concept and in the absence of a long history of implementation of the relevant rules, *CDS 3.0* calls for additional protections which grant service providers the peace of mind to engage with the new framework. Legal 'safe harbours' are one such form of protection that grants immunity to enforcement by other persons or regulators as long as certain formal criteria have been satisfied.[67]

In Australia's Consumer Data Right, the 'safe harbour' provisions can be found in Section 56GC of the *CCA*, which grants immunity from any proceedings (whether civil or criminal) to any CDR participant, provided that it acts in good faith in compliance with the Act, the relevant regulations and *CDR Rules*. Section 56GC protects both data holders and accredited data recipients and understandably places an evidential burden of proof on these businesses, as they should 'know whether or not they received evidence of a valid consent or request and otherwise met the obligations in the CDR regime.'[68]

Overall, the safe harbour protections in Section 56GC are a welcome driver of service providers' participation in the CDR ecosystem and do not appear problematic per se. At the same time, the interests of CDR participants protected by it need to be weighed against the potential implications for customers whose data these participants exchange. In Chapter 5, we argue that the safe harbour can generate substantial risks, by facilitating unauthorised disclosures of CDR data and shifting the liability for omissions made by service providers towards the customer.

4.5 Data quality, usability and financial incentives

The interests of incumbent service providers controlling the 'silos' of customer data deserve a separate analysis in the light of their perceived lack of motivation to participate in third-generation *CDS* frameworks. Indeed, while the recipients of customer data (such as fintechs and other service providers) clearly stand to benefit from a *CDS 3.0* regime, their counterparts who share that data lose their privileged position and seemingly do not gain any apparent benefit in return.

Lack of self-interest may cause data holders to treat *CDS* rules as a compliance exercise and limit their engagement with the *CDS 3.0* ecosystem and associated capital expenditure. The likely consequences of this status quo include poor quality and usability of data shared with potential competitors. Furthermore, the possibility that a holder of customer data can also act as a data recipient within the *CDS 3.0* ecosystem (e.g., by obtaining corresponding authorisation as an ADR in Australia), gives rise to a free-rider problem: the same entity acting as a data holder is not incentivised to *contribute* high quality data to the *CDS 3.0* ecosystem, but has a strong interest in free-riding by *extracting* high quality data through the same ecosystem when acting as a data recipient.

Even where service providers are genuinely interested in promoting the *CDS 3.0* ecosystem by contributing high quality data, their confidence in their own compliance efforts can be undermined by legal uncertainty. As an example, different stakeholders may interpret their duties differently if the scope of their data quality obligations is not explained with sufficient precision. The Consumer Data Right in Australia is no exception: a 2023 consultation on data quality in the CDR highlighted the need for better guidance and clarifications on data quality-related obligations in the CDR framework,[69] prompting the ACCC to publish its Clarification of Specific Data Quality Obligations.[70]

Availability of alternative data sharing methods like screen-scraping (see Section 4.3) further complicates things and may incentivise data holders to take shortcuts. Indeed, a simple solution to the above conundrum is to reduce the reliance on the *CDS 3.0* ecosystem and induce customers to provide their data directly through less secure channels. This happens in Australia, where some accredited data recipients have continued to rely on screen-scraping despite obtaining formal authority from the ACCC to receive data through CDR channels. From the perspective of development of the *CDS 3.0* ecosystem, this outcome is highly undesirable, since both groups of service providers facilitating the exchange of customer data (holders and recipients) end up having the *motivation* and *tools* to circumvent the CDR regime.

One possible solution to the lack of meaningful incentives for data holders involves giving them the right to charge the recipients for the shared data. However, this creates another complication, which goes against the pro-competition objectives of *CDS 3.0*: the position of data holders as gatekeepers becomes further entrenched and the costs of processing customer data escalate (and are likely passed on to customers) – which could effectively stall the development of the *CDS 3.0* ecosystem. Australia's Consumer Data Right seeks to address this issue through built-in flexibility. On the one hand, sectoral designations may specify 'each of the classes of information within the designated information for which a person may charge a fee.'[71] On the other hand, there is a clear expectation that such instances should be rare and the costs minimal:

> It is anticipated that the majority of designated data sets would be made available for free. Only in rare circumstances, for example, where the marginal cost of disclosure would be significant, would it be appropriate for a data set to be designated as a chargeable data set.[72]

The emergence of a specialist group of service providers – data aggregators (discussed in Section 2.1) – adds further complexity to *CDS 3.0* dynamics, which may well incentivise monopolisation due to the inherent economies of scale. While these specialist service providers may be better motivated to focus on the quality and usability of customer data, the magnitude of the underlying risks to competition has invited proposals to impose 'a universal access requirement designed to ensure that data aggregators cannot unreasonably deny incumbent financial institutions, fintech disruptors, or their customers access to their platforms.'[73]

Lastly, a discussion about the quality and usability of customer data would be incomplete without considering its implications for data portability and its main beneficiary – the customer. While it is easy to become lost among the competing concerns of the different service providers, we argue that *CDS 3.0* frameworks, regardless of specific design features, must enable customers, as the originators of valuable data circulating within the *CDS 3.0* ecosystem, to free-ride by having direct access to high quality data they can trust (as discussed in Section 5.2.4). This helps view *CDS 3.0* not only through the important competition lens, but also as a tool enabling customers to take *direct control* of the data they generate – which provides stronger motivation for policymakers to be more actively involved in monitoring the quality of customer data and enforcing any violations.

This final observation stresses the importance of weighing the interests of service providers against those of their customers. A poor balance may substantially undermine *consumer trust* – a complex concept in *CDS 3.0* that deserves its own chapter in this book. We turn to it now.

Notes

1 *Directive (EU) 2015/2366 of the European Parliament and of the Council of 25 November 2015 on Payment Services in the Internal Market, Amending Directives 2002/65/EC, 2009/110/EC and 2013/36/EU and Regulation (EU) No 1093/2010, and Repealing Directive 2007/64/EC* [2015] OJ L 337/35, art 5(1)(e) (*'PSD2'*).
2 Ibid art 5(1)(f).
3 Ibid art 5(1)(g).
4 For example, account information service providers must register with the Financial Conduct Authority ('FCA') unless they already hold a broader authorisation

under the *Payment Services Regulation 2017* (UK). Applicants must satisfy the criteria listed in that regulation: reg 17 sch 2. See also OBIE, *Open Banking for Read/Write Participants* (2018) 3–4. See also Treasury, Australian Government, *Review into Open Banking: Giving Customers Choice, Convenience and Confidence* (Report, December 2017) 16, 22, 24 (*'Review into Open Banking'*).

5 *Competition and Consumer (Consumer Data Right) Rules 2020* (Cth) rr 1.9, 5.12 (2)(a) (*'CDR Rules'*).
6 Ibid r 5.12(1)(a).
7 Ibid r 5.12(1)(b).
8 Ibid r 5.12(1)(c).
9 Ibid r 5.12(2)(b).
10 Ibid rr 1.7 (definition of 'addresses for service'), 5.12(d)–(e).
11 See, e.g., ibid sch 2.
12 Anton Didenko, 'Australia's Consumer Data Right and Its Implications for Consumer Trust' (2024) 50(1) *Monash University Law Review* (forthcoming) 18–21 <https://ssrn.com/abstract=4543464>.
13 *CDR Rules* (n 5) rr 5.17–19.
14 *Review into Open Banking* (n 4) recommendation 2.8; Advisory Committee on Open Banking, *Final Report of Advisory Committee on Open Banking* (Report, April 2021) 20 <www.canada.ca/content/dam/fin/consultations/2021/acob-ccsbo-eng.pdf>.
15 See Raiz Invest Limited, Submission No 29 to Senate Select Committee on Financial Technology and Regulatory Technology, *Inquiry into the FinTech and RegTech Sectors* (24 December 2019) 6 <www.aph.gov.au/Parliamentary_Business/Committees/Senate/Financial_Technology_and_Regulatory_Technology/Financial-RegulatoryTech/Submissions?main_0_content_1_RadGrid1ChangePage=2_20v> ('Raiz Submission').
16 Parliament of Australia, *Senate Select Committee on Financial Technology and Regulatory Technology* (Interim Report, September 2020) 137 [5.27]. See also 'Raiz Submission' (n 15) 6; Madison Utley, 'ACCC Amends Open Banking for Brokers: But It's Not Enough', *Australian Broker News* (Web Page, 7 December 2020) <www.brokernews.com.au/news/breaking-news/accc-amends-open-banking-for-brokers-but-its-not-enough-274629.aspx>.
17 Thus, 'sponsored' participants cannot collect customer data from the data holder. Instead, their 'sponsors,' who are participants at an unrestricted level, collect customer data on their behalf. See *CDR Rules* (n 5) r 7.4(2) and Section 1.7 above.
18 Australian Government, *Accreditation Guidelines* (Version 4, December 2022) 28–9.
19 See, e.g., Basiq, 'Statutory Review of the Consumer Data Right' (Issues Paper, 10 June 2022) <https://treasury.gov.au/sites/default/files/2022-09/c2022-314513-basiq.pdf>.
20 See, e.g., Xero, Submission to Treasury, *Consumer Data Right Statutory Review* (20 May 2022) 3 <https://treasury.gov.au/sites/default/files/2022-09/c2022-314513-xero.pdf>.
21 Australian Government, *Statutory Review of the Consumer Data Right* (Report, 2022) 48–50 <https://treasury.gov.au/sites/default/files/2022-09/p2022-314513-report.pdf>.
22 *Review into Open Banking* (n 4) 23.
23 *Competition and Consumer Act 2010* (Cth) ss 56CG-CH, 56CE (*'CCA'*). See also ACCC, Submission to Treasury, *Statutory Review of the Consumer Data Right* (May 2022) 2 <https://treasury.gov.au/sites/default/files/2022-09/c2022-314513-australian_competition_and_consumer_commission.pdf>.

24 Mortgage & Finance Association of Australia, Submission to Treasury, *Inquiry into Future Directions for the Consumer Data Right* (18 May 2020) 3 <https://treasury. gov.au/sites/default/files/2020-07/mortgage-finance-association.pdf>.

25 Deloitte, Submission to ACCC, *Consumer Data Right Rules Framework* (12 October 2018) 9–10 <www.accc.gov.au/system/files/CDR%20-%20Rules%20-%20 Submission%20to%20framework%20-%20Deloitte%20-%20PUBLIC%20VERSION.pdf>.

26 Financial Planning Association of Australia, Submission to Treasury, *Inquiry into Future Directions for the Consumer Data Right* (21 May 2020) 1 <https://treasury. gov.au/sites/default/files/2020-07/fpa-australia.pdf>.

27 Westpac, Submission to Treasury, *Inquiry into the Future Directions for the Consumer Data Right* (25 May 2020) 8 <https://treasury.gov.au/sites/default/ files/2020-07/Westpac-2020.pdf> (emphasis added).

28 Australian Privacy Foundation, Submission to Treasury, *Inquiry into the Future Directions of the Consumer Data Right* (6 May 2020) 2 <https://treasury.gov.au/ sites/default/files/2020-07/australian-privacy-foundation.pdf> (emphasis added).

29 Financial Rights Legal Centre, Submission to Treasury, *Inquiry into Future Directions for the Consumer Data Right* (May 2020) 45 <https://treasury.gov.au/sites/ default/files/2020-07/c2020-62639-financialrightslegalcentre.pdf> (emphasis added). See also Financial Rights Legal Centre, Submission to ACCC, *CDR Rules Expansion Amendments Consultation Paper* (October 2020) 29 <https://financial-rights.org.au/wp-content/uploads/2020/10/201029_ACCCCDRRulesexpansion_ Sub_FINAL-1.pdf>.

30 Consumer Policy Research Centre, Submission to ACCC, *Consumer Data Right Rules Framework* (12 October 2018) 3–4 <www.accc.gov.au/system/files/ CDR%20-%20Rules%20-%20Submission%20to%20framework%20-%20Consumer%20Policy%20Research%20Centre%20-%20PUBLIC%20VERSION.pdf>.

31 Treasury, Australian Government, *Future Directions for the Consumer Data Right: Consumers; Choice; Convenience; Confidence* (Report, October 2020) 111 <https://treasury.gov.au/sites/default/files/2021-02/cdrinquiry-final.pdf> (emphasis added).

32 See *Competition and Consumer (Consumer Data Right) Amendment Rules (No 1) 2021* (Cth) *Competition and Consumer (Consumer Data Right) Amendment Rules (No 1) 2021* (Cth) sch 3.

33 See ibid sch 3 para 5; *CDR Rules* (n 5) r 1.10C(2).

34 For more detail, see Anton Didenko, *Implications of the Consumer Data Right Framework for Trusted Advisers* (Report for CPA Australia, March 2022) <www.cpaaustralia.com.au/-/media/project/cpa/corporate/documents/tools-and-resources/business-management/consumer-data-right-report-2022.pdf?rev=99a9f de22c7e4c8bbbc36fe395ddd0f3&download=true>.

35 *CDR Rules* (n 5) r 1.10AA.

36 Ibid.

37 Ibid r 1.10AA(2)(d).

38 Ibid r 1.16A(1); *CCA* (n 23) s 56BL.

39 *CDR Rules* (n 5) r 1.10A(9).

40 Note, however, that under the CDR regime, 'CDR business consumers' cannot directly share their data with 'CDR representatives': see ibid rr 1.10AA(1)(a), 10A(1)(c)(v), 1.10A(10).

41 Explanatory Statement, Competition and Consumer (Consumer Data Right) Amendment Rules (No 1) 2023 (Cth).

42 As noted at n 40 above, 'CDR business consumers' cannot directly share their data with 'CDR representatives'.

43 This section is based on the paper by Natalia Jevglevskaja and Ross P. Buckley, 'Screen Scraping in Australian Finance' (2023) 42(2) *The University of Queensland Law Journal* 277.
44 See *Privacy Act 1988* (Cth) pt IIIA; *National Consumer Credit Protection Act 2009* (Cth) pt 3-2CA.
45 ABA, *Code of Banking Practice* (at 5 October 2021).
46 For further detail on the problem of SS, see below, Section 5.2.2. See also Jevgleskaja and Buckley (n 43).
47 Advisory Committee on Open Banking, *Final Report* (Report, April 2021) <www.canada.ca/content/dam/fin/consultations/2021/acob-ccsbo-eng.pdf>.
48 Financial Data Exchange is a non-profit, industry standards body, dedicated to unifying financial services around a common, secure, and interoperable technical standard for user-permissioned sharing of financial data: see 'About FDX', *Financial Data Exchange* (Web Page) <https://financialdataexchange.org/FDX/FDX/About/About-FDX.aspx?hkey=dffb9a93-fc7d-4f65-840c-f2cfbe7fe8a6>.
49 Financial Data Exchange, Comments to Consumer Financial Protection Bureau (2020) 9 <https://finledger.com/wp-content/uploads/sites/5/2021/03/Financial-Data-Exchange-Comments-to-CFPB.pdf>.
50 FinTech Australia, Submission No 182 to Productivity Commission, *Inquiry into Data Availability and Use: Open Financial Data* (August 2016) 4; *Review into Open Banking* (n 4) 51, 72.
51 'Why Connecting to Open Banking APIs Is Not as Simple as It Seems', *Tink Blog* (Blog Post, 19 August 2021) <https://tink.com/blog/open-banking/complexities-behind-open-banking-connections/>.
52 Ibid.
53 Ibid. See also Andrei Cazacu, 'PSD2: Does Europe Need a Single API Standard?', *TrueLayer* (Blog Post, 13 July 2022) <https://truelayer.com/blog/psd2-does-europe-need-a-single-api/>.
54 Account information services collate information on a customer's multiple bank accounts in a single place (providing a consolidated overview of the financial situation) allowing the consumer to better manage personal finances. Payment initiation services facilitate online payments. See, e.g., *PSD2* (n 1) preamble, paras 28–9.
55 World Bank, 'Open Banking: Comparative Study on Regulatory Approaches' (Technical Note, 2022) 21. See also Inna Oliinyk and William Echikson, *Europe's Payments Revolution: Stimulating Payments Innovation while Protecting Consumer Privacy* (Research Report No 2018/06, September 2018) 3 <www.ceps.eu/wp-content/uploads/2018/09/RR2018_06_Europes%20Payments%20Revolution.pdf>.
56 'What Are the Differences between Open Banking and Screen Scraping?', *Adatree* (Web Page, 1 February 2021) <https://adatree.com.au/2021/02/01/what-are-the-differences-between-open-banking-screen-scraping/>.
57 Ruth Wandhöfer, 'Title IV, Chapter 5 "Operational and Security Risks and Authentication" (Arts 95–98)', cited in Gabriella Gimigliano and Marta Božina Beroš, *The Payment Services Directive II: A Commentary* (Edward Elgar, 2021) 192–3 [12.020]; Financial Data Exchange, *ABCs of the APIs* (Organisation Overview, 29 August 2019) 5 <https://finledger.com/wp-content/uploads/sites/5/2021/03/ABCs_of_APIs_FINAL_1-1.pdf>.
58 PTJ Wolters and BPF Jacobs, 'The Security of Access to Accounts Under the PSD2' (2019) 35(1) *Computer Law and Security Review* 35.
59 Australian Government, *Statutory Review of the Consumer Data Right* (Report, 2022) 31 (*'CDR Statutory Review'*).
60 See Ralf Ohlhausen, 'The EBA Is Wrong About Screen Scraping, and How It Will Hurt European Fintech!', *inFinite Intelligence* (23 March 2017) <www.

finextra.com/blogposting/13865/the-eba-is-wrong-about-screen-scraping-and-its-going-to-hurt-european-fintech>.

61 *Review into Open Banking* (n 4) 52.

62 Ibid 10.

63 Tonia Berglund, 'From Screen Scraping to Open Banking', *Australian Broker* (Web Page, 1 July 2021) <www.brokernews.com.au/features/opinion/from-screen-scraping-to-open-banking-277582.aspx>.

64 *CDR Statutory Review* (n 59) 31. See also FinTech Australia, Submission No 19 to Senate Select Committee on Financial Technology and Regulatory Technology, *Australia as a Technology and Financial Centre* (September 2019) 35.

65 Illion, Submission to Treasury, Parliament of Australia, *Inquiry into Future Directions for the Consumer Data Right* (11 May 2020) <https://treasury.gov.au/sites/default/files/2020-07/illion.pdf> 5.

66 Senate Select Committee on Financial Technology and Regulatory Technology, Parliament of Australia, *Interim Report* (Report, September 2020) [5.57].

67 Safe harbours are used (albeit with mixed success) as a regulatory tool across different areas of the law, from intellectual property, to insolvency, to data privacy, to competition. See, e.g., Danny Friedmann, 'Sinking the Safe Harbour with the Legal Certainty of Strict Liability in Sight' (2014) 9(2) *Journal of Intellectual Property Law & Practice* 148; Craig Edwards, 'Australia's Safe Harbour Law: A Better Outcome for Restructuring and Entrepreneurship?' (2019) 27(2) *Insolvency Law Journal* 66; Yann Padova, 'The Safe Harbour Is Invalid: What Tools Remain for Data Transfers and What Comes Next?' (2016) 6(2) *International Data Privacy Law* 139; OECD Directorate for Financial and Enterprise Affairs Competition Committee, 'Safe Harbours and Legal Presumptions in Competition Law' (Background Note by the Secretariat, DAF/COMP(2017)9, 9 November 2017) <https://one.oecd.org/document/DAF/COMP(2017)9/en/pdf>.

68 Explanatory Memorandum, Treasury Laws Amendment (Consumer Data Right) Bill 2019 (Cth) [1.472] 78 ('Treasury Laws Memorandum').

69 ACCC, *Data Quality in the Consumer Data Right: Findings from Stakeholder Consultation* (Report, 5 April 2023) 15 <www.accc.gov.au/system/files/Data-Quality-in-the-Consumer-Data-Right-Findings-from-Stakeholder-Consultation.pdf>.

70 ACCC Regulatory Guidance, 'Clarification of Specific Data Quality Obligations', *Consumer Data Right* (Web Page, 26 June 2023) <https://cdr-support.zendesk.com/hc/en-us/articles/7044968934799-Clarification-of-specific-Data-Quality-obligations>.

71 *CCA* (n 23) s 56AC(2)(D).

72 Treasury Laws Memorandum (n 68) [1.55] 14.

73 Dan Awrey and Joshua Macey, 'The Promise and Perils of Open Finance' (2023) 40(1) *Yale Journal on Regulation* 1, 7.

Chapter 5

Customer perspective: the quest for customer trust

Abstract

This chapter analyses the impact of *CDS 3.0* frameworks on customers by focusing on the concept of customer trust. *Section 5.1* explains why customer trust is a critical component of a healthy *CDS 3.0* ecosystem and highlights its institutional, impersonal nature. *Section 5.2* identifies two preconditions for customer trust – *risk* and *interdependence* – to build a taxonomy of different enablers of customer trust in a *CDS 3.0* ecosystem. It acknowledges that despite sharing the same motivation for engaging with the *CDS* ecosystem, various customers can be affected differently by the relevant *interdependencies* and may have vastly different capacity to deal with the associated *risks*. To consider a wider range of trust-enabling factors, *Sections 5.2.1–5.2.5* focus on five key enablers of customer trust from the perspective of *individual consumers* as the most vulnerable group of customers.

5.1 Necessity of customer trust for CDS 3.0

Customer engagement with the *CDS 3.0* ecosystem depends on multiple factors, such as the level of awareness of its prospective benefits, availability of alternative data sharing methods, the attractiveness of use cases for customer data developed by service providers or the complexity of the *CDS* software platform's user interface. The underlying reasons can be financial, technical and even psychological but, despite their differences, all are united by a common goal to build and maintain *customer trust*. The latter is crucial for *CDS 3.0* for three main reasons.

The first one is obvious. Despite the central role of service providers in building the infrastructure (the 'pipes') for the sharing and processing of customer data, in the absence of customer engagement there is nothing to share or process. In other words, without customer trust, a *CDS 3.0* framework lacks its object (customer data) and purpose. *CDS 3.0* seeks to *empower* customers to direct the flow of their data by giving them better tools to exercise control over it and harvest its value. The decision to use *CDS 3.0* channels or rely on alternative data sharing methods[1] remains in the hands of the customer, as the *CDS 3.0* ecosystem is designed around *voluntary interaction* of customers

DOI: 10.4324/9781003414216-5

with different service providers. Such interaction is impossible if customers do not trust that *CDS 3.0* works to their benefit.

Second, customer trust in a *CDS 3.0* framework is *institutional* and *impersonal*: customers do not need to trust each individual or business involved in the circulation of their data and can rely on the system as a whole. The mechanics of this kind of trust are explained well by Gillespie et al: 'If we go on board a commercial aircraft or if we hand in our savings to a bank, we do not trust these pilots or bankers as individuals, but rather representatives of complex "expert systems." '[2] A *CDS 3.0* framework is just another kind of 'expert system': customers cannot be expected to perform due diligence on each service provider including the reliability of their computer platforms and personnel.

Incidentally, a similar logic applies to ecosystems developed for the circulation of money. Scholars have relied on the inherent economic value of customer data as the basis to establish, convincingly, 'the *functional equivalence* of customer data and customer funds as valuable information.'[3] If we accept this analogy, we should also recognise that the value of money in the economy mainly depends on the level of trust in the relevant currency[4] – and conclude that *CDS 3.0* as a system for the transfer of valuable customer information should follow a similar logic.

Lastly, the cross-sectoral nature of *CDS 3.0* frameworks elevates the role of customer trust and creates complex dynamics.[5] On the one hand, successful implementation in one sector (e.g., in finance) could boost the level of trust customers place in the entire ecosystem and positively affect other sectors. On the other hand, a reverse effect is equally plausible: high-profile breaches of customer data in other sectors may impact the customers' perception of *CDS 3.0* in finance. As a result, customer trust can be particularly hard to maintain in a multi-sectoral setting since the loss of trust in one sector can quickly spread to others.

5.2   Enablers of customer trust in *CDS 3.0* frameworks

The dynamic, changing nature of customer trust suggests that it can increase or decline over time, depending on a range of factors that either enable or inhibit it. These factors will be the focus of the current section, after we briefly establish what trust means and how it is created.[6]

Interdisciplinary scholarship defines trust as 'a psychological state comprising the intention to accept vulnerability based upon positive expectations of the intentions or behavior of another.'[7] Two preconditions must be satisfied for trust to emerge: (i) *risk* (risk creates an opportunity for trust, which leads to risk taking) and (ii) *interdependence* (the interests of one party cannot be achieved without reliance upon another).[8]

The duality of risk and interdependence helps to identify the different enablers of customer trust in a *CDS 3.0* framework briefly summarised in Table 1.1.[9]

Table 1.1 Enablers of customer trust in a CDS 3.0 framework

Enabler of customer trust	Risk	Interdependence
Accreditation	Inability to verify the trustworthiness of recipients of customer data	Customers rely on the regulators and the accreditation mechanism to assess the trustworthiness of the recipient of customer data
Information security and privacy	Mismanagement of customer data by its recipient and unauthorised access to customer data	Customers rely on recipients of customer data to maintain its safety and integrity
Customer redress	Inability to obtain recourse from recipients of customer data when the CDS 3.0 ecosystem fails to prevent loss or damage to customers	Customers rely on the availability of redress mechanism and the recipient's capability to provide sufficient compensation
Customer empowerment	Inability to obtain direct access to customer data in convenient machine-readable form through secure data channels	Customers rely on the efficiency of the data sharing process (including speed of response to customer requests and usability of customer data) and safety of data channels used to share customer data with the customer
Customer experience and awareness	Inadequate understanding of the underlying risks and limitations of the CDS 3.0 framework	Customers rely on limited interactions with the CDS 3.0 processes (like consent management) and expect the CDS 3.0 ecosystem to be safe and reliable

Before proceeding with our analysis, we must acknowledge that despite sharing the same motivation for engaging with a *CDS 3.0* ecosystem, various customers can be affected differently by the relevant interdependencies and may have vastly different capacity to deal with the associated risks. As an example, sophisticated business customers and individual consumers will typically have incomparable levels of expertise and financial resources. The impact of data breaches on the two groups will vary as well.

To deal with this conundrum, the following discussion in Section 5.2.1–5.2.5 will focus on each of the five enablers of customer trust, emphasising, where relevant, the perspective of *individual consumers as the most vulnerable group of customers*. While it is true that the effects of the different factors mentioned in Table 1.1 on other customers may be less impactful, pragmatism suggests that individual consumers and their distinctive vulnerabilities should inform the design of *CDS 3.0* ecosystems, at least at an early stage. The incidental opportunity of more sophisticated customers to free-ride on the additional protections and features developed for the more vulnerable groups should not negatively affect the latter. If necessary, certain individual consumer-specific features can be 'switched off' for other customers. The evolution of Australia's *CDS 3.0* regime supports this conclusion. Although the Consumer Data Right launched as a highly restrictive framework, subsequent amendments – such as the reduced data sharing restrictions for customer data of 'CDR business consumers'[10] – have relaxed the regulatory parameters for more sophisticated customers. We argue therefore that our focus on individual consumers in the remaining sections of this chapter provides an excellent opportunity to consider a wider range of trust-enabling factors, risks and interdependencies.

The five enabling factors of customer trust below are listed in no particular order. This is intentional, as we lack the empirical evidence to weigh and compare them. Each of these factors contributes to the creation of institutional trust in the *CDS 3.0* ecosystem *as a whole*. At the same time, we hypothesise that failure to acknowledge and consider even a single one of these factors may have a disproportionate effect on customer trust and squander the potential for trust built by the others. As an illustration, we anticipate that a major data breach in a *CDS 3.0* ecosystem can nullify the perceived benefits of having a simple customer interface, just as difficulties with enforcing customer rights to obtain compensation can nullify the perceived benefits of prescribed data security obligations.

5.2.1 Accreditation

For the customer, accreditation in Australia's CDR framework serves as a signpost of reliability and the capacity of recipients of CDR data to comply with their obligations. Its value to the customer is explained by several factors. Accreditation is impartial, as it is issued by regulators, rather than the market, and thus constitutes an important advantage of the CDR as a mandated *CDS 3.0* regime. In contrast to other important features of the CDR, such as specific information security controls discussed in Section 5.2.2, accreditation offers enhanced visibility: anyone may consult the list of persons accredited by the ACCC.[11] Accessibility coupled with ease of use make accreditation a powerful enabler of customer trust and arguably the *only* tool less sophisticated customers can rely on considering the vast information asymmetry between individual consumers and accredited service providers.

By comparison, compliance with individual accreditation requirements[12] is much more difficult for non-experts to verify. Information security controls[13] can be evaluated only by having access to the computer systems of accredited persons; evaluation of the 'fit and proper person criteria'[14] requires access to information about their key personnel; while the effectiveness of the dispute resolution[15] systems can only be meaningfully tested on an *ex post* basis when a conflict has arisen (at which point it is arguably too late as the data is already shared with the (un)accredited person). Against this background, we expect most customers to rely instead on the broad powers of the ACCC to monitor accredited businesses and, where necessary, suspend or revoke accreditation[16] and impose or vary its conditions.[17]

For as long as all recipients of customer data in a *CDS 3.0* ecosystem must be accredited, accreditation gives rise to an attractive proposition: such recipients can be trusted because they are *trustworthy*. This connotation was reflected in the Treasury's 2019 overview of the Consumer Data Right:

> Consumers will *only* be able to use the right to direct the transfer of their data to *trusted* third parties. *All* data recipients who receive consumer specific data must be accredited.[18]

This clear and straightforward overview matched the original design of the CDR framework at its launch in 2020, at which point all recipients of CDR data indeed had to be accredited. However, the introduction of exemptions for so-called 'trusted advisers' in 2021 (as explained in Section 4.2) changed the paradigm. Accreditation stopped being the exclusive pathway enabling access to CDR data. For some recipients, it became sufficient to belong to one of the prescribed groups of professional advisers: (i) qualified *accountants*[19]; (ii) persons admitted to the *legal profession*; (iii) registered *tax agents, BAS agents* and *tax (financial) advisers*[20]; (iv) *financial counselling agencies*[21]; (v) 'relevant providers' within the meaning of the *Corporations Act 2001* (Cth)[22]; and (vi) mortgage brokers.[23]

This reform diminished the role of accreditation as a source of customer trust in the CDR ecosystem. From a customer's perspective, this presented a challenge: can accreditation be effectively substituted by an equally compelling trust enabler, and if so, which one? An attempt to respond to this challenge and defend the reform was made in the explanatory statement to the amending legislation.[24] Upon review, we find the CDR's response to this challenge unconvincing for two reasons.

Our first criticism is that the rhetoric in the explanatory statement is not adequately supported by the revised CDR rules.

On the one hand, it suggests that disclosure of CDR data to unaccredited advisers is acceptable because they represent 'professions that are considered to be appropriately regulated to receive CDR data, particularly due to consumer protection mechanisms that form part of their regulatory framework.'[25] In other words, despite lack of accreditation these recipients should be deemed trustworthy as regulated professionals. While an attractive proposition at first glance, this does not explain what is considered 'appropriately regulated.' Are the regulatory standards applicable to 'trusted advisers' higher, equal to or lower than those applicable to accredited persons? After all, if 'appropriately regulated' means 'equally or better regulated,' then clearly any further explanation would be unnecessary. Unfortunately, if we put aside the explanatory statement and start analysing the revised CDR framework, we must conclude this is not the case.

Disclosures to trusted advisers are subject to consumer experience standards,[26] which require the entity disclosing CDR data to such trusted advisers to 'state that data disclosed to a non-accredited person will *not* be regulated as part of the Consumer Data Right' and 'advise the consumer to review how the non-accredited person will handle their data.'[27] It follows that it is the customer's responsibility to investigate what regulatory standards or policies may or may not apply to the trusted adviser. Here, the CDR framework applies a hands-off approach to CDR data in the hands of trusted advisers and does not attempt to address any discrepancies in the levels of regulatory protections available to customers – which could be significant. By inviting customers to protect themselves if and when necessary, the CDR regime creates a semblance of 'caveat emptor': let the customers beware of any risks at their own peril. This, in our view, does nothing to boost customer trust in the CDR ecosystem. The difference between formal accreditation supported by regulatory oversight, on the one hand, and an invitation for customers (and particularly individual consumers) to do their own due diligence, on the other, is massive, and the abstract rhetoric in the explanatory statement that trusted advisers should be deemed 'appropriately regulated' is unhelpful.

Our second criticism relates to the mechanics of disclosing CDR data to trusted advisers. Even if trusted advisers were subject to the same regulatory standards as accredited data recipients, customers cannot easily verify whether the recipient of their data is accredited by consulting a public register maintained by the ACCC. Instead, they must rely on the good faith of the disclosing entity, which is only required to take '*reasonable steps* to confirm that a person nominated as a trusted adviser was, and remains, a member of a class' of trusted advisers.[28] While such disclosing entity benefits from the 'safe harbour' provisions mentioned in the previous chapter,[29] customers may end up unprotected in the event of third-party mistakes, as discussed in Section 5.2.3.

Furthermore, we argue that the average individual consumer is unlikely to comprehend the true extent of the explanatory statement's argument that 'disclosure of the CDR data from an accredited data recipient to a trusted adviser is covered by the information security controls'[30] – which, as we discussed in Section 2.2.3, is rather limited as the relevant protections do not apply to CDR data *at rest* (i.e., any CDR data held by the trusted adviser).

This brings us to the third and final criticism – reliance on trust customers already have (or should have) in trusted advisers and the assumption that the existing trust is sufficient. A key feature of the trusted adviser reform is that it does not add *any* new basis for customer trust whatsoever. The discussion above suggests the whole premise of the reform is to *free-ride* on whatever trust customers may already have in so-called 'trusted advisers.' It does not matter whether such trust is warranted or misplaced, and if such trust does not exist in the first place, then it should originate somewhere else. We argue that reliance on external sources of customer trust can be short-sighted for several reasons.

First, evidence of past breaches of regulatory controls suggests that the claims that 'trusted advisers' are 'appropriately regulated' may well be overstated. A 2018 study by the Australian Securities and Investments Commission (ASIC) revealed that in a vast majority (75%) of examined cases advisers failed to comply with their best interests duty.[31] A later study similarly revealed massive levels of non-compliance exceeding 50%.[32] In addition, it is not sufficient to establish that professional advisers are subject to bespoke rules, codes and standards without assessing their effectiveness and impact on customers. ASIC's recent first-ever court proceedings against RI Advice Group Pty Ltd for alleged breach of applicable cyber security rules provide a good illustration.[33] The regulator relied on a vaguely drafted obligation to 'do all things necessary to ensure that the financial services covered by the licence are provided efficiently, honestly and fairly'[34] to establish the existence of specific cyber security obligations – which ended up being highly problematic considering the lack of detailed regulatory guidance.[35] Here, the existence of applicable rules was not in doubt – but their exact scope proved to be elusive even in court, let alone on an ex ante basis.

Second, while it may be true that consumers 'routinely share their banking data with . . . these professionals,'[36] it appears unrealistic to expect most of them to have sufficient expertise and insider knowledge to verify compliance of trusted advisers with any applicable duties, codes or standards.

Third, since professional advisers offer specialist knowledge and expertise, customers may feel pressured to use their services despite any concerns about the safety of their data: '[i]n reality most people who rightly (or wrongly) trust their advisor will simply do what the so-called trusted advisor will ask of them to do.'[37]

Reliance on pre-existing trust alone gives rise to another issue: the revised CDR framework for trusted advisers offers no meaningful incentives for such advisers to compete among themselves and improve their internal data management and information security processes. If those processes do not match the CDR standards, there is no reason to bridge the gap – thereby propagating the boundary issue of having a two-track system for the sharing of the same customer data.[38] As discussed previously in Section 2.2.3, the latter outcome is unsatisfactory and calls for the unification of relevant standards economy-wide. These criticisms are even stronger following the recent amendments enabling disclosures of CDR data of 'CDR business consumers' to unaccredited persons that are not 'trusted advisers' (see Section 4.2.5).

In the wider context, the above discussion illustrates a conflict between different priorities in the development of *CDS 3.0* frameworks. In Australia's

Consumer Data Right, the considerations of promoting customer trust, while clearly present, were secondary to the main function of the reforms: expanding participation in the CDR framework. We eagerly await to see how a similar conundrum will be resolved in future *CDS 3.0* regimes elsewhere.

5.2.2   Information security and privacy

Security and privacy of customer data is a cornerstone of Australia's Consumer Data Right. The 2022 statutory review (Statutory Review) recognised 'strong privacy requirements' as a 'foundation of trust' in the CDR framework.[39] The CDR introduces a set of bespoke Privacy Safeguards[40] that switch on and off at different points in the lifecycle of CDR data.[41] The complex interaction between the Privacy Safeguards and the 'general' privacy legislation represented by the APPs was discussed in Section 2.2.3. For the purposes of this chapter, however, we stress that the positive impact of the Privacy Safeguards on customer trust can be linked to the increased level of customer protection afforded by the Privacy Safeguards observed in stakeholder submissions to the Statutory Review:

> When compared to the Australian Privacy Principles (APP) established under the Privacy Act 1988, many submissions noted the CDR's Privacy Safeguards afford a higher level of protection for consumers than the APP, reflecting the increased volume and accessibility of personal information under the scheme.[42]

More specifically, Privacy Safeguard 12 (security of CDR data, and destruction or de-identification of redundant CDR data)[43] requires accredited data recipients to 'take the *steps specified in the consumer data rules* to protect the CDR data from . . . misuse, interference and loss; and . . . unauthorised access, modification or disclosure.'[44] These steps are: (i) to '[d]efine and implement security governance in relation to CDR data,' (ii) to '[d]efine the boundaries of the CDR data environment,' (iii) to '[h]ave and maintain an information security capability,' (iv) to '[i]mplement a formal controls assessment program' and (v) to '[m]anage and report security incidents.'[45] These more specific provisions are further supported by standards made by the Data Standards Chair about the security of CDR data, including 'authentication of CDR consumers to a standard which meets, in the opinion of the Chair, best practice security requirements.'[46]

The information security controls in the CDR ecosystem largely remain technology-neutral and offer flexibility to accommodate different levels of cyber risks. The information security capability of an accredited data recipient must be '*appropriate and adapted* to respond to risks to information security,' having regard, among other things, to the extent and nature of cyber threats to CDR data and potential loss or damage to one or more CDR consumers in case of a data breach.[47] In addition, an ADR 'must review and adjust its information security capability' at least annually – as well as 'in response to material changes to both the nature and extent of threats and its CDR data environment.'[48]

A flexible approach to information security risks is aligned with international practices[49] and recognises that recipients of valuable data may differ substantially in terms of business size, financial resources and cyber resilience. In other words, smaller businesses can be expected to have less sophisticated information security controls. While attractive in terms of regulatory pragmatism, this approach may be objectionable from the perspective of individual consumers, who we take to be far less interested in the inner workings of service providers holding their valuable data. In the case of a cyber event leading to loss of particularly sensitive information (such as data enabling identity fraud) most customers will not (and should not) care whether their data was in the hands of a small fintech company or a major bank.

This raises the difficult question about an acceptable minimum level of information security controls in a *CDS 3.0* framework and the criteria that determine that minimum level. While we expect to see different approaches across *CDS 3.0* regimes in the future, we argue that the *types of data* held by service providers in a *CDS 3.0* ecosystem should be no less important than the size, capability of such businesses or other incidental factors that are largely inconsequential from the perspective of building customer trust. We argue that the information security controls of recipients of valuable customer data may need to be adjusted depending on types of customer data held by them, with stronger protections required from businesses handling information which may cause long-term harm to consumers (such as identity fraud) in the event of a breach. The proposed approach can be summarised as 'same data, same risks, same controls.' Considering the risks of loss of customer data and the lack of agreed best practices for *CDS 3.0*, we argue our approach will help curb the immediate risks of increased data circulation among smaller, less sophisticated businesses – at least upon initial launch of *CDS 3.0* frameworks.

The principle 'same data, same risks, same controls' can help address the boundary problem caused by the application of different rules to the same customer data depending on a technicality – such as whether the data is in transit to a trusted adviser or at rest (see Section 2.2.3). It is noteworthy that the wholesale exemption of trusted advisers from the CDR framework in Australia has created more than two information security regimes for CDR data. Since different advisers are subject to different rules, the resulting status quo is a *mixture of different regimes*: one for ADRs and six regimes for the six categories of trusted advisers; plus the multitude of information security regimes applicable to other non-accredited service providers that are permitted to receive CDR data upon authorisation from 'CDR business consumers' (see Section 4.2.5). The resulting patchwork of information security regimes is vulnerable to the 'weakest link' risk generated by entities with the lowest information security controls. Once this is accepted, it comes as no surprise that some stakeholders in Australia have argued that '[w]ithin seconds . . . a customer's data will travel from *the most secure setting at the bank* to *no or uncertain security with Trusted Advisers.*'[50] The above reference to poor or uncertain security of some holders of customer data is a perfect segue to another challenge: the practice of screen-scraping, which was discussed in Section 4.3 from the service providers' perspective. This section, on the contrary, focuses on customers. Although stakeholders recognise the Consumer Data Right framework 'as a more secure system for data sharing than other channels like screen-scraping,'[51] at the time of writing the latter remains a valid alternative to the CDR in Australia, which may inhibit customer trust for several reasons.

First, as noted by the US Treasury, the mechanics of screen-scraping facilitate fraud and cyber risks.[52] There are no accepted standards for screen-scraping, and customers who use this method are likely to breach the terms and conditions of their service provider.[53] Furthermore, 'legal screen scraping can be hard to distinguish from illegal automation, like malicious bots or credential stuffing'[54] – which forces financial institutions to adopt radical measures like whitelisting IP addresses of known data aggregators since the latter 'simply cause too much traffic for the fraud prevention teams to effectively investigate.'[55] Such a blunt approach lacks precision but is explained by its greater efficiency: in some cases, '[data] aggregators represent up to 25% of financial institutions' total traffic – something that would take fraud prevention teams [years] to analyze manually if not safe-listed by their bot detection tools.'[56]

Second, even if we accept screen-scraping as a necessary evil that enables customers to harvest the value of their data more quickly and easily, albeit with additional risks, the introduction of *CDS 3.0* changes the status quo and creates powerful incentives to abolish this practice. This is reflected in Scott Farrell's review into the future directions for the CDR in Australia, which concluded that 'eventual prohibition of the practice of screen scraping for payment initiation would be in the interests of consumers,'[57] as well as the Statutory Review, which noted that screen-scraping 'should be banned in the near future in sectors where the CDR is a viable alternative.'[58]

More importantly, screen-scraping, if left unattended, may create perverse incentives for service providers operating in a *CDS 3.0* ecosystem. As long as such businesses are free to pursue screen-scraping, transition to *CDS 3.0* may be delayed substantially. We have observed this in Australia, where businesses have argued that ASIC should not interfere on the grounds that the Consumer Data Right 'is not yet at a stage where it is considered by the industry as a viable alternative to "screen scraping" and other forms of digital data capture of such value as to outweigh the regulatory costs of participating in the CDR framework.'[59] Furthermore, the same businesses may simply opt to maintain *both* streams of customer data.

The ability to use screen-scraping as an extra tool in the arsenal of service providers should not be dismissed due to the apparent conflict of interest it creates. It follows, we argue, that direct regulatory intervention is warranted. It is thus reassuring to note that at the time of writing, it appears likely the Australian government will announce a ban on screen-scraping within the coming year. This ban is expected to be implemented following an extended transition period during which industry can implement the CDR as a superior alternative practice. This reinforces our conclusion in Section 2.1 that a more efficient *CDS 3.0* ecosystem needs to be supported by a prescriptive legal framework.

5.2.3   Customer redress

CDS 3.0 aims to increase the volume of customer data exchanged between different service providers.[60] The associated risks (including cyber risks) multiply and are more likely to materialise and cause damage to customers. This simple realisation stresses the importance of enabling customers to obtain recourse. In contrast to accreditation,[61] which helps generate customer trust *ex ante* (i.e., prior to giving consent to share data with the accredited person), the ability of customers to obtain redress for breaches of the applicable rules is crucial *ex post*. The reason is simple. If the customer has suffered damage from the actions of a service provider in a *CDS 3.0* ecosystem, it follows that accreditation has failed to achieve its purpose. Prevention should give way to remediation.

In Australia's Consumer Data Right framework, customer remediation is based on the process of litigation, which is supported by professional insurance obligations of accredited data recipients. The underlying complexity warrants a separate discussion, which will follow in Chapter 6. For the purposes of this section, however, it is necessary to acknowledge that the matter of customer redress can conflict with the interests of service providers – which may lead to undesirable consequences for customers, as illustrated by the analysis of the CDR's 'safe harbour' provisions. As shown below, in the CDR framework safe harbours have a dual effect. On the one hand, they offer added protection and certainty to service providers.[62] On the other hand, this result is effectively achieved by offloading the residual risks onto customers. Instead of eliminating business risks, safe harbours merely reallocate them.

As discussed in Section 4.4, the 'safe harbour' in Section 56GC of the *CCA*, grants immunity from legal proceedings to any CDR participant, provided it acts in good faith in compliance with the Act, the relevant regulations and *CDR Rules*. In the light of the preceding discussion about the challenges of accreditation, let us consider the effects of this provision on customers in the context of disclosures of CDR data to trusted advisers.

As mentioned in Section 5.2.1, the primary rationale for the abolition of accreditation requirements for trusted advisers was the assumption that as regulated professionals they should already be trustworthy without interference from the CDR regime. It follows that the *identity* of a trusted adviser should be the key enabler of customer trust since a disclosure to an entity that is neither accredited nor regulated as a trusted adviser may leave the customer (in particular, individual consumer) unprotected. The role of customers in transfers to trusted advisers is limited to giving consent to authorise the disclosure. The latter is performed by service providers (in this case – ADRs). But what if an ADR makes a mistake? The *CDR Rules* create a fiction:

> Where the accredited person has taken *reasonable steps* to confirm that a person nominated as a trusted adviser was, and remains, a member of a [relevant] class . . . , the person is taken to be a member of that class for the purposes of this rule.[63]

Coupled with Section 56GC of the *CCA* (the 'safe harbour'), this provision effectively creates a shield for ADRs, which only need to demonstrate a minimal degree of competence in identifying the recipient of customer data. According to the explanatory statement, the 'reasonableness' test here employs 'a *scalable standard* that will depend on the circumstances.'[64] The absence of clear criteria that must be satisfied can be problematic for ADRs, which may struggle to determine ex ante what 'reasonable steps' they need to take to obtain protection.[65] Unfortunately, the implications for customers are more substantial: as long as service providers are able to obtain legal protection of the 'safe harbour,' CDR data may *lawfully* end up in the hands of an unaccredited third party who is not a trusted adviser – with no opportunity to obtain recourse.

To our knowledge, the application of the safe harbour provision has not been tested in courts. But the risks for customers and implications for customer trust are apparent and cannot be ignored: we hypothesise that most customers would expect the professional service provider – that is, an ADR – to be accountable for *any* mistake made during disclosure of CDR data. The unfortunate, and likely unintended, result of an understandable attempt to give peace of mind to participating service providers is that customers end up bearing residual responsibility for the omissions of those service providers. This outcome appears unsatisfactory given the significant information asymmetry between the customer and the ADR: the former are 'unlikely to know whether a particular action by an entity breaches their privacy rights' in the first place.[66]

Since the safe harbour merely rebalances the risks in favour of service providers, it gives rise to a conflict of interests: service providers are rewarded for *formal* compliance, whereas customers must deal with *any* mistakes, regardless of their service providers' degree of competence. We argue that this outcome is inappropriate for a customer-oriented *CDS 3.0* framework that relies on customer trust to operate: customers should not bear the residual responsibility for the actions or inactions of their service providers.

Protection of customers from the negative effects of safe harbour provisions can be an important step towards a more customer-oriented *CDS 3.0* framework. At the same time, we expect that certain jurisdictions may choose to implement more substantial customer protections. One such mechanism – an obligation for recipients of customer data to use such data in the best interests of the customer – has been proposed recently by Australia's competition watchdog.[67]

The idea of establishing an overarching duty in a *CDS 3.0* framework has been floated outside Australia, with some experts arguing that '[a]s soon as an entity starts dealing with a consumer's data, a fiduciary responsibility should be created, and this should apply irrespective of whether the entity is regulated or not.'[68] In recent years, scholars have helpfully highlighted the importance of data-related fiduciary obligations as enablers of customer trust.[69] In theory, these obligations, if applied economy-wide, could help address some of the limitations of the boundary problem discussed in Section 5.2.2 and reinforce the principle 'same data, same risks, same controls.' They can also help overcome the limitations of safe harbours which, as we noted earlier in this section, de facto reinforce formal compliance but inadvertently transfer business risks to customers. The scope and content of fiduciary obligations for *CDS 3.0* frameworks can vary significantly from country to country and deserve a separate analysis, including consideration of related risks, such as the risk of 'imposing an excessive regulatory burden' in certain sectors.[70] Such analysis, however, is beyond the scope of this book.

5.2.4   Customer empowerment

As a *CDS 3.0* framework, Australia's Consumer Data Right seeks to empower customers by enabling them to make better use of their data. Despite the importance of the enabling technology (such as APIs) and its use by the service providers, the customer remains in control. The CDR cannot function without the customer's consent, which must be (i) voluntary, (ii) express, (iii) informed (iv) specific as to purpose, (v) time limited and (vi) easily withdrawn.[71] The customer must voluntarily choose to engage with the *CDS 3.0* ecosystem, which is highly unlikely without customer trust in the CDR framework as a whole.

Customer empowerment in the CDR is not limited to elevating the role of customer consent. It can take many forms, some of which we find questionable – such as the customer's responsibility for investigating which regulatory standards or policies may or may not apply to the trusted adviser (see Section 5.2.1). Another important form of customer empowerment is the customer's ability to receive data about themselves, in a usable format, directly from the service provider, otherwise known as data portability (see Section 1.3) – a feature which has been described in the Statutory Review as 'a key part of CDR objects' with 'totemic significance'[72] but remains disabled at the time of writing.

'Direct-to-customer' disclosure refers to the process of sharing CDR data directly with the customer – thus enabling the latter to use the data as it chooses. This form of disclosure is clearly envisaged in the CDR's statutory objective 'to enable consumers . . . to require information relating to themselves . . . to be disclosed safely, efficiently and conveniently . . . *to themselves* for use as they see fit.'[73] Despite its apparent significance for the Consumer Data Right, this basic data portability functionality was disabled at launch and was subsequently deferred in 2021 'pending a future consultation process.'[74] The 2022 Statutory Review concluded 'it is in the interest of consumers that this function remain disabled' for reasons such as low consumer literacy and lack of capacity to make use of CDR data.[75] We hypothesise this decision may also be at least partially explained by the absence of clear tangible benefits for service providers, which may understandably find the 'direct-to-customer' pathway commercially unattractive.[76]

We argue that the restricted portability of CDR data in Australia represents a lost opportunity to build customer trust in the Consumer Data Right and can be interpreted by customers as a deficiency in the CDR framework. It is difficult to reconcile with the CDR's hands-off approach to screen-scraping, which remains unconstrained at the time of writing. As a result, the status quo appears to represent an immature Consumer Data Right regime, rather than a tribute to customer incompetence. Furthermore, the problem of insufficient customer literacy appears exaggerated when we recall the operative term 'consumer' in the CDR framework is not limited to individuals, who may indeed lack the capacity to make full use of CDR data. As discussed in Section 2.2, the word 'consumer' in the CDR regime covers corporations as well. Once we add this into the equation, the decision to 'switch off' direct-to-customer data portability *for everyone* seems unnecessary. After all, as discussed in Section 4.2.5, the recent changes have sought to empower some of the CDR consumers, known as 'CDR business consumers' by granting them the right to share their CDR data with *any* unaccredited persons. However, if some of the customers governed by Australia's Consumer Data Right framework are now permitted to share their CDR data freely at their own risk, there appears to be no good reason to deny them the right to receive a copy of their CDR data. Lastly, we argue that lack of meaningful financial incentives for service providers should not be relevant for data portability: in an efficient *CDS 3.0* framework customers *should* be able to *free-ride* on the financial incentives generated by the portability and interoperability of their data (see Section 1.3).

More importantly, we argue that 'direct-to-customers' data sharing in a *CDS 3.0* framework should not necessarily replicate the mechanics of disclosures to trusted advisers whereby the CDR 'switches off' completely when the CDR data reaches the relevant adviser. A more refined approach is needed to enable customers to benefit from the protections afforded by *CDS 3.0*, directly access the data and easily verify its accuracy. Considering the real risk that individual consumers may indeed become the 'weakest link' in a chain of transfers of their data, we propose a two-step process for this group of customers (which may be extended to all customers if practicable).[77] Step one involves copying customer data to a secure regulated environment (a 'direct-to-customers' hub) to maintain the custody and safety of customer data. Step two involves providing customers with the credentials to access such CDR data when needed. We argue this approach offers several important advantages.

First, this approach overcomes the limitations or malfunctions of customers' personal data storage devices (computers, mobile phones) and enables customers to access their data at any time. Second, it effectively limits customer-generated risks to unauthorised access to their data, which can be mitigated through common information security controls like multi-factor authentication; while the central hub of customer data benefits from industrial-grade cyber resilience. Third, compared to screen-scraping, unauthorised access to the central hub offers limited benefits to attackers: the latter will only be able to obtain access to certain data instead of full control of a customer's bank account. This outcome should not change upon the introduction of action initiation[78]: we expect the central hub to be used only for storage of customer data to enable easier data portability, whereas action initiation functionality will be part of data interoperability.[79] Fourth, our proposed approach avoids the current limitations of reciprocity in the CDR regime, whereby not all recipients of CDR data are legally obligated to share the customer data held by them pursuant to a customer's request: by using the central hub the customer can circumvent the limitation and share their data directly with whoever they choose.

A foreseeable downside of the proposed approach is the concentration of vast amounts of customer data within the central hub, which is likely to make the hub an attractive target for cyber criminals. Our response is two-pronged. First, we expect the hub will be regulated and required to implement best-in-class information security controls that exceed not only an individual consumer's level of cyber resilience, but also the average level of information security among the service providers in the CDR ecosystem. Second, in the event of cyber incidents, customers should be able to obtain redress for actions or omissions of the hub's operator.[80] At the same time, in the interests of fairness, customers should remain answerable for damage caused by unauthorised access to the central hub resulting from a customer's own failure to ensure the safety of their login credentials.[81] Policymakers should also be aware of the 'gateway risk' that operators of the central hub may abuse its position as controller of vast amounts of customer data. This issue is yet another argument in favour of establishing a mandated model of *CDS 3.0* to ensure strict regulatory controls and oversight of operators of the proposed central hub.

5.2.5   *Customer experience and awareness*

Overall complexity, limited awareness and other factors negatively affecting customer experience may significantly undermine customer trust in a *CDS 3.0* framework, making it inaccessible for large groups of customers – particularly individual consumers:

> Friction and high cognitive load can cause consumers to disengage before they obtain any value – only the most committed persist.[82]

Commentators have described consumer experience as 'a critical driver of success' for the Consumer Data Right in Australia,[83] and the overall level of attention to the process of customer engagement with the CDR ecosystem is very high. This is illustrated by the development of bespoke Consumer Experience Standards[84] and Consumer Experience Guidelines.[85] Accessibility and ease of use are rightly seen as enablers of customer interaction with the CDR framework and appear largely uncontroversial.

In contrast, customer awareness presents a dilemma. On the one hand, it can serve as a powerful enabler of customer trust: only those customers who understand the mechanics of the *CDS 3.0* regime can fully appreciate its benefits and recognise its limitations – and, as a result, make a genuinely informed decision to engage with the *CDS 3.0* ecosystem. On the other hand, information overload can lead to consumer fatigue[86] and come into conflict with the twin notions of simplicity and accessibility which enhance customer experience. A balance needs to be struck between the two competing factors. In this section, we explore how to achieve this balance.

Empirical data regarding the level of customer engagement with Australia's Consumer Data Right remains limited at the time of writing but our observations strongly suggest that the level of customer awareness of the CDR is very limited.[87] This comes as no surprise, considering that '88% of Australian consumers do not have a clear understanding of how their personal information is being collected and shared.'[88] These unimpressive numbers suggest that better awareness of the CDR mechanics could help promote customer trust and, in turn, customer engagement with the Consumer Data Right: 'If customers are unaware that they have this right, or if they feel insufficiently protected in exercising that right, customers may lack the incentive to participate.'[89]

At the same time, since the regulatory resources are limited and empirical data remains limited, costly awareness campaigns can be hard to justify. This can explain why the Statutory Review considers raising public awareness a matter of lower regulatory priority:

> Consumer education and technical understanding are *unlikely* to be the core drivers of consumer adoption, and the focus should be on building the CDR brand as a trusted form of data sharing, a *trust mark* of sorts, and to provide the warning signs of unsafe practices.[90]

Considering these limitations, awareness campaigns should focus on issues of particular importance and immediate impact. These issues will be jurisdiction-specific, dictated by the design choices made by the developers of *CDS 3.0* frameworks. However, the preceding discussion in this chapter helpfully illustrates the importance of customer trust as enabler of voluntary engagement with a *CDS 3.0* regime. We argue therefore, that, as a minimum, customers should be aware of any risks and deficiencies in a *CDS 3.0* framework that may be *detrimental to their interests*.

By way of example, in Australia the issues that deserve greater customer awareness would include the following. First, the differences in levels of customer protection within the CDR ecosystem and outside its boundaries, and the overall complexity associated with disclosures to trusted advisers need to be clearly explained – and establish clearly when and why the *same* CDR data is regulated and protected *differently*.[91] Second, we find the rhetoric used to describe certain professional advisers as 'trusted' ultimately unhelpful and potentially misleading: however attractive linguistically, the term 'trusted adviser' creates a potentially misleading connotation that the relevant professional advisers are de facto *trustworthy*, whereas the CDR regime adopts a hands-off approach to the relevant risks and even invites consumers to investigate and protect themselves against the relevant risks.[92] Third, customers should be aware that the safe harbour provisions enable service providers to fail to comply with the customers' instructions and escape all liability as long as such providers have made a reasonable effort to comply in good faith.[93] More generally, we argue customers should at least be informed about all situations when their CDR data can be *lawfully misused without any liability to the customer*.

We admit that raising customer awareness of the above risks may not sound particularly attractive from the perspective of promoting voluntary participation in a *CDS 3.0* framework and its overall health. After all, the level of customer trust reflects the current *perception* of the *CDS 3.0* ecosystem – which may well be distorted: trust may exist when the customer is not aware of the full extent of the risk. This may give policymakers a perverse incentive not to draw additional attention to certain risks in order to preserve customer trust. We argue this approach would be short-sighted in the long term, since trust built on insufficient customer awareness of the relevant risks has a shaky foundation. If any of the relevant risks eventually materialise, we anticipate the negative fallout resulting from the sudden realisation of the extent of those risks will exceed any short-term benefits resulting from keeping customers in the dark.[94]

Lastly, better customer awareness of the relevant risks can be a useful tool to prevent policymakers from integrating into CDS 3.0 frameworks any rules which may be detrimental for customers. The important task of identifying those rules may well fall to academia and consumer organisations as independent and competent adjudicators.

Notes

1 See Section 4.3.
2 Nicole Gillespie et al., 'Restoring Institutional Trust After the Global Financial Crisis: A Systemic Approach' in Roderick M Kramer and Todd L Pittinsky (eds), *Restoring Trust in Organizations and Leaders: Enduring Challenges and Emerging Answers* (Oxford University Press, 2012) 185, 193.
3 Scott Farrell, 'Banking on Data: A Comparative Critique of Common-Law Open Banking Frameworks' (PhD Thesis, UNSW Sydney, 2022) iii (emphasis added); Scott Farrell, *Banking on Data: Evaluating Open Banking and Data Rights in Banking Law* (Wolters Kluwer, 2023) ch 3.
4 According to the Reserve Bank of Australia, 'money derives its value from the trust people place in it': 'What Is Money?', *Reserve Bank of Australia* (Web Page) <www.rba.gov.au/education/resources/explainers/what-is-money.html>. For a comprehensive discussion about the nature of money, see Benjamin Geva, *The Payment Order of Antiquity and the Middle Ages: A Legal History* (Hart Publishing, 2011); Simon Gleeson, *The Legal Concept of Money* (Oxford University Press, 2018).
5 Trust is a dynamic phenomenon having multiple phases. One taxonomy identifies a building phase, a stability phase and a dissolution phase. See Denise Rousseau et al., 'Not So Different After All: A Cross-Discipline View of Trust' (1998) 23(3) *Academy of Management Review* 393, 396.
6 Analysis in this section expands upon the following research: Anton Didenko, 'Australia's Consumer Data Right and Its Implications for Consumer Trust' (2024) 50(1) *Monash University Law Review* (forthcoming) ('Australia's Consumer Data Right').
7 Rousseau et al. (n 5) 395.
8 Ibid.
9 Adapted from Didenko, 'Australia's Consumer Data Right' (n 6).
10 See Sections 2.2.2(b), 4.2.5.
11 See 'Current Providers', *Consumer Data Right* (Web Page) <www.cdr.gov.au/find-a-provider>.
12 See *Competition and Consumer Act 2010* (Cth) ss 56BB(d), 56BH ('*CCA*').
13 See Sections 2.2.3 and 5.2.2.
14 *Competition and Consumer (Consumer Data Right) Rules 2020* (Cth) rr 1.9, 5.12(2)(a) ('*CDR Rules*').
15 Ibid rr 5.12(1)(b)–(c).
16 Ibid r 5.17.
17 Ibid r 5.10.
18 Treasury, Australian Government, *Consumer Data Right Overview* (Report, September 2019) 7 <https://treasury.gov.au/sites/default/files/2019-09/190904_cdr_booklet.pdf> (emphasis added).
19 As defined in *Corporations Act 2001* (Cth) ss 9 (definition of 'qualified accountant'), 88B ('*CA*').
20 As defined in *Tax Agent Services Act 2009* (Cth).
21 As defined in *Corporations Regulations 2001* (Cth) reg 7.6.01(7).
22 This group includes certain individuals authorised to provide personal advice to retail clients. See Explanatory Statement, Competition and Consumer (Consumer Data Right) Amendment Rules (No 1) 2021 (Cth) 19 ('2021 Explanatory Statement').
23 As defined in *National Consumer Credit Protection Act 2009* (Cth) ss 5 (definition of 'mortgage broker'), 15B.

24 2021 Explanatory Statement (n 22) 18.
25 Ibid.
26 *Competition and Consumer (Consumer Data Right) Amendment Rules (No 1) 2021* (Cth) sch 3 cl 12 (*'CDR Amendment Rules 2021'*); *CDR Rules* (n 14) r 8.11(1)(c) (iv). For more detail about the different categories of consumer experience standards, see 'Consumer Experience', *Consumer Data Standards* (Web Page) <https://consumerdatastandardsaustralia.github.io/standards/#consumer-experience>. Customer experience is further discussed in Section 5.2.5.
27 See 'Consumer Experience: Consent Standards', *Consumer Data Standards* (Web Page) <https://consumerdatastandardsaustralia.github.io/standards/#consumer-experience> (emphasis added).
28 *CDR Amendment Rules 2021* (n 26) sch 3 cl 5; *CDR Rules* (n 14) r 1.10C(3) (emphasis added).
29 See Section 4.4.
30 2021 Explanatory Statement (n 22) 20.
31 ASIC, *Financial Advice: Vertically Integrated Institutions and Conflicts of Interest* (Report No 562, January 2018) 36 <https://download.asic.gov.au/media/4632718/rep-562-published-24-january-2018.pdf>. The 2021 Explanatory Statement (n 22) expressly mentions best interests duties as evidence that 'trusted advisers' are subject to regulatory oversight but does not clarify how such general duties might help protect customers under the Consumer Data Right framework. We hypothesise these duties may be of some use in dealing with conflicts of interest between customers and CDR data recipients, which is crucial in the context of enforcement, as discussed in Section 5.2.3.
32 ASIC, *Financial Advice by Superannuation Funds* (Report No 639, December 2019) 30 <https://download.asic.gov.au/media/5395538/rep639-published-3-december-2019.pdf>.
33 *Australian Securities and Investments Commission v RI Advice Group Pty Ltd* [2022] FCA 496 (*'RI Advice'*).
34 *CA* (n 19) s 912A(1)(a).
35 *RI Advice* (n 33) [46]–[47].
36 Consumer Data Right, Australian Government, 'CDR Rules Expansion Amendments' ('Consultation Paper, September 2020) 30 <www.accc.gov.au/system/files/CDR%20rules%20expansion%20amendments%20-%20consultation%20paper%20-%2030%20September%202020.pdf>.
37 Financial Rights Legal Centre, Submission to Australian Competition and Consumer Commission, *Consultation on Proposed Changes to the Consumer Data Right Rules* (October 2020) 32 <https://financialrights.org.au/wp-content/uploads/2020/10/201029_ACCCCDRRulesexpansion_Sub_FINAL-1.pdf>.
38 See Section 2.2.3.
39 Treasury, Australian Government, *Statutory Review of the Consumer Data Right* (Report, 2022) 4 <https://treasury.gov.au/sites/default/files/2022-09/p2022-314513-report.pdf> (*'Statutory Review'*).
40 Privacy Safeguards are accompanied by corresponding data standards.
41 See Section 2.2.3.
42 *Statutory Review* (n 39) 17.
43 *CCA* (n 12) s 56EO.
44 Ibid (emphasis added).
45 *CDR Rules* (n 14) sch 2 cl 7.11.
46 Ibid r 8.11.
47 Ibid sch 2 cl 1.5 (Step 3).
48 Ibid.
49 For more detail, see, e.g., Anton N Didenko, 'Cybersecurity Regulation in the Financial Sector: Prospects of Legal Harmonization in the European Union and Beyond' (2020) 25(1) *Uniform Law Review* 125.

50 ABA, Submission to Treasury, *Consumer Data Right Rules Amendments (Version 3)* (30 July 2021) 2 (emphasis added) <https://treasury.gov.au/sites/default/files/2021-10/aba.pdf>.

51 *Statutory Review* (n 39) 17.

52 United States Department of the Treasury, *A Financial System That Creates Economic Opportunities: Nonbank Financials, Fintech, and Innovation* (Report to President Donald J Trump, July 2018) 34 <https://home.treasury.gov/sites/default/files/2018-08/A-Financial-System-that-Creates-Economic-Opportunities-Non-bank-Financials-Fintech-and-Innovation.pdf> (emphasis added) (citations omitted). See also Jeffrey Voas et al., 'Cybersecurity Considerations for Open Banking Technology and Emerging Standards' (Paper, Draft NISTIR 8389, January 2022) <https://nvlpubs.nist.gov/nistpubs/ir/2022/NIST.IR.8389-draft.pdf>.

53 Reserve Bank of Australia, Submission to Treasury, *Inquiry into Future Directions for the Consumer Data Right* (Issues Paper, 23 April 2020) 3 <https://treasury.gov.au/sites/default/files/2020-07/rba.pdf>.

54 Olov Renberg, 'Fintech Aggregators and Open Banking: Service Enablers or an Unfortunate Backdoor for Fraud?', *Security Boulevard* (Web Page, 8 December 2021) <https://securityboulevard.com/2021/12/fintech-aggregators-and-open-banking-service-enablers-or-an-unfortunate-backdoor-for-fraud/>.

55 Ibid.

56 Ibid.

57 Treasury, Australian Government, *Inquiry into Future Directions for the Consumer Data Right* (Report, October 2020) 97 <https://treasury.gov.au/sites/default/files/2021-02/cdrinquiry-final.pdf>.

58 *Statutory Review* (n 39) 12.

59 ASIC, *Response to Submissions on CP 341 Review of the ePayments Code: Further Consultation* (Report No 718, March 2022) [115] 34.

60 See, e.g., Treasury, Australian Government, *Strategic Assessment: Outcomes* (Report, January 2022) <https://treasury.gov.au/sites/default/files/2022-01/p2022-242997-outcomes-report_0.pdf>.

61 See Section 5.2.1.

62 See Section 4.4.

63 *CDR Amendment Rules 2021* (n 26) sch 3 3 para 5; *CDR Rules* (n 14) r 1.10C(3) (emphasis added).

64 2021 Explanatory Statement (n 22) 19 (emphasis added).

65 This outcome is perhaps ironic, considering that the key purpose of a safe harbour is to give comfort to service providers through increased legal certainty.

66 Maddocks, *Australian Competition and Consumer Commission: Consumer Data Right Regime; Update 2 to Privacy Impact Assessment* (Report, 8 February 2021) 59 <www.accc.gov.au/system/files/CDR%20-%20Update%202%20to%20privacy%20impact%20assessment.pdf>.

67 ACCC, Submission to Treasury, *Statutory Review of the Consumer Data Right* (June 2022) <https://treasury.gov.au/sites/default/files/2022-09/c2022-314513-australian_competition_and_consumer_commission.pdf> ('ACCC Submission').

68 Elevandi, *Open Finance and Beyond Roundtable* (Report, 2023) 4 <www.elevandi.io/wp-content/uploads/2023/02/Elevandi-Insights-Forum_Open-Finance-And-Beyond-Roundtable-Report.pdf>.

69 See, e.g., Ariel Dobkin, 'Information Fiduciaries in Practice: Data Privacy and User Expectations' (2018) 33(1) *Berkley Technology Law Journal* 1; Jack Balkin, 'The Fiduciary Model of Privacy' (2020) 134(1) *Harvard Law Review Forum* 11.

70 ACCC Submission (n 67).

71 *CDR Rules* (n 14) r 4.9.

72 *Statutory Review* (n 39) 25.

73 *CCA* (n 12) s 56AA(a)(i) (emphasis added).

74 Treasury, Australian Government, 'Developments in Australia's Consumer Data Right in Response to Community Feedback' (Media Release, 30 April 2021) <https://treasury.gov.au/media-release/developments-australias-consumer-data-right-response-community-feedback>.
75 *Statutory Review* (n 39) 25–7.
76 See also Section 4.5.
77 There appears to be no convincing policy reason to deny the more sophisticated customers the right to obtain a copy of their data using other formats.
78 See Section 3.2.
79 The difference between data portability and interoperability is discussed in Section 1.3.
80 See Section 5.2.3 and Chapter 6.
81 Australia's ePayments Code can be used as a reference point for determining the types of circumstances in which the user is liable for unauthorised access: see ASIC, 'ePayments Code' (2 June 2022) ch C.
82 *Statutory Review* (n 39) 43.
83 Data Standards Body and Consumer Policy Research Centre, 'Stepping Towards Trust' (Report, August 2020) 4 <https://cprc.org.au/wp-content/uploads/2021/12/CPRC-Consumer-Data-Standards-Consumer-Data-Rights-Report-1.pdf>.
84 See 'Consumer Experience', *Consumer Data Standards* (Web Page) <https://consumerdatastandardsaustralia.github.io/standards/#extensibility>.
85 See ibid.
86 For more detail, see, e.g., George Milne, Andrew Rohm and Shalini Bahl, 'Consumers' Protection of Online Privacy and Identity' (2004) 38(2) *Journal of Consumer Affairs* 217.
87 Natalia Jevglevskaja and Ross P. Buckley, 'The Consumer Data Right: How to Realise This World-Leading Reform' (2022) 45(4) *UNSW Law Journal* 1589, 1620–1.
88 'CPRC 2020 Data and Technology Consumer Survey', *Consumer Policy Research Centre* (Web Page, 7 December 2020) <https://cprc.org.au/publications/cprc-2020-data-and-technology-consumer-survey/>.
89 Treasury, Australian Government, *Review into Open Banking: Giving Customers Choice, Convenience and Confidence* (Report, December 2017) 9–10.
90 *Statutory Review* (n 39) 39 (emphasis added).
91 Disclosures to 'CDR business consumers,' which were introduced into the CDR framework in 2023, appear largely uncontroversial, as they are aimed at the more sophisticated category of customers: see Section 4.2.5.
92 See Section 5.2.1.
93 See Sections 4.4 and 5.2.3. See also Chapter 6.
94 Our conclusion finds indirect support in the work of Muzatko and Bansal, who revealed, in the context of data breaches, that 'companies that delay the announcement of a data breach are likely to suffer a *larger drop in consumer trust* than those companies that immediately disclose the data breach.' See Steven Muzatko and Gaurav Bansal, 'Timing of Data Breach Announcement and ECommerce Trust' (Study, MWAIS 2018 Proceedings, 2018) (emphasis added).

Chapter 6

Enforcement: efficiency and fairness

Abstract

This chapter focuses on the enforcement challenges of *CDS 3.0* regimes. *Section 6.1* explains why ease of enforcement of customer rights is crucial in a *CDS 3.0* ecosystem. *Section 6.2* highlights the limitations of relying on mandatory insurance as a regulatory tool to boost customer confidence in *CDS 3.0* – and argues that mandatory insurance needs to be supplemented by additional measures that remain effective in the event of bankruptcy of the party which handles the processing of customer data.

6.1 Ease of enforcement

In the previous chapter, we established that redress serves as an important enabler of customer trust in *CDS 3.0* frameworks when other elements of those frameworks (such as accreditation or information security requirements) have failed to prevent damage to the customer.[1] In this section, we explore in greater detail why the process of enforcing customer rights in a *CDS 3.0* regime needs to be simplified and why compensation is the superior form of enforcement of customer rights in *CDS 3.0*, mainly on the grounds of efficiency and fairness.

6.1.1 'Assume breach'

We start with information security – a battleground between cyber attackers and their targets. Compared to other operational threats facing service providers handling customer data, cyber threats possess several distinctive characteristics. They are generated by motivated and often highly trained attackers, which makes cyber risks notoriously difficult to predict and mitigate. These threats do not simply persist in one form – they evolve over time, demanding a more elaborate response to match their increased sophistication. It is therefore unsurprising that cyber threats require a different response that is 'based on the realistic assumption that not all attacks can be prevented.'[2] This response

DOI: 10.4324/9781003414216-6

follows the logic of 'assume breach,' which prioritises responding to cyber breaches instead of attempting to construct invulnerable cyber fortresses. The futility of relying exclusively on cyber risk *prevention* is widely accepted, even in the most regulated and technically sophisticated sectors of the economy like banking. In its Financial Stability Review published in October 2021, the Reserve Bank of Australia went so far as to conclude that 'a significant cyber event that has the potential for systemic implications is at some point *inevitable*.'[3] Outside finance, any sector with large volumes of valuable information can be expected to face a similar status quo. In Australia, this conclusion can be illustrated by the extraordinary chain of major cyber breaches in the second half of 2022, which impacted major businesses in tele- communications (Optus),[4] insurance (Medibank),[5] retail (Woolworths)[6] – and prompted an urgent and substantial increase of penalties for data breaches.[7] Half a year later, in May 2023, the Australian Government 'made the decision to *pause expansion* [of the Consumer Data Right] into superannuation, insur- ance and telecommunications.'[8] While causation is hard to prove, the tim- ing of the change, the acknowledgment that 'further time is needed to allow the CDR to mature' and the decision to 'focus on ensuring that the CDR in banking is working as effectively as possible' suggests the 2023 changes and the 2022 data breaches are related. Regardless of the actual reasons for this change, the importance of the 'assume breach' logic for the Consumer Data Right has been expressly acknowledged by stakeholders: the Australian Pri- vacy Foundation has argued that '[d]ata breaches are a near certainty' and the real question one should be concerned about 'is not if but when.'[9]

The impact of the 'assume breach' logic on *CDS 3.0* frameworks is pro- found. If end-users and policymakers accept that every entity, regardless of accreditation, size or other criteria, will experience a cyber incident sooner or later, the role of accreditation and various information security controls aiming to *prevent* the loss of valuable customer data is diminished. If safety of customer data cannot be guaranteed in a *CDS 3.0* ecosystem, whose func- tion is to facilitate the sharing of that data with various service providers, then depriving the customer of meaningful recourse *ex post* (i.e., after the breach) is grossly *unfair*, since the customer bears the resulting risks, includ- ing identity theft. For this reason, we argue, all *CDS 3.0* frameworks should incorporate mechanisms enabling customers to obtain recourse in the event of cyber incidents affecting their data. The *efficiency* of such mechanisms will depend on their design, as discussed below, by reference to Australia's CDR framework.

6.1.2 Direct claim against service providers

We argue that, as a minimum, customers should have a right to make a direct claim against a service provider in a *CDS 3.0* ecosystem for damage caused by its action or failure to act, for several reasons. First, this form of redress may be unavailable under the general privacy law, since not all customer data covered by the *CDS 3.0* framework may qualify as eligible *personal information* (e.g., if the data relates to a business, rather than an individual). Second, the process of obtaining redress by customers may be constrained by various formalities preventing *direct* enforcement. The implementation of the CDR in Australia illustrates these limitations and supports our earlier hypothesis that a *CDS 3.0* framework can serve as a 'testing laboratory' for new data sharing rules before extrapolating them to the rest of the economy (see Section 2.2.3).

Upon the CDR's launch in 2020, Australia's *Privacy Act 1988* (Cth) offered limited options to initiate litigation for breaches of privacy, each an *indirect* multi-stage process. Generally, the process of obtaining recourse includes three steps.[10] First, individuals complain to the Information Commissioner[11] about an act or practice that may be an interference with the privacy of the individual.[12] Second, the Information Commissioner finds the complaint substantiated and makes a determination including a declaration that the complainant is entitled to a specified amount by way of compensation.[13] Third, only then the complainant may commence proceedings in court for an order to enforce a determination.[14] Furthermore, the definition of 'personal information' only covers information about *individuals* (rather than businesses).[15]

To overcome these limitations, Australia's Consumer Data Right introduced a *statutory right of action* which enables customers who suffer loss or damage by an act or omission of another person in contravention of the Privacy Safeguards or the consumer data rules to 'recover the amount of the loss or damage by action against that other person or against any person involved in the contravention.'[16] Notably, this right of action does not require the preliminary steps envisaged in the general privacy legislation and thereby greatly simplifies enforcement by making it less time consuming. Several years later, in February 2023, in his Privacy Act Review Report the Attorney-General proposed 'to allow for a direct right of action in order to permit individuals to apply to the courts for relief in relation to an interference with privacy.'[17] The change has not been implemented at the time of writing, and the proposal envisages at least one intermediary step before proceedings can be initiated (claimant would first need to make a complaint to the OAIC and have their complaint assessed for conciliation either by the OAIC or a recognised EDR [external dispute resolution] scheme]).[18] As a result, the CDR's direct right of action remains the superior form of customer redress.

Despite its apparent advantages, the statutory right of action has limitations. These limitations, as we argue in the next subsection, should prompt *CDS 3.0* frameworks to establish a more efficient process for customers to obtain compensation.

6.1.3   Preconditions of efficient customer compensation

By itself, the direct right of action granted to customers in a *CDS 3.0* framework may have limited usefulness for several reasons.

First, the associated time and financial costs can be unduly burdensome for less sophisticated customers, such as individual consumers. The latter have limited capacity to sue service providers efficiently due to inequalities in bargaining power and information asymmetries.[19]

If the higher frequency of transfers of valuable customer information in a *CDS 3.0* ecosystem or the market concentration dynamics[20] of *CDS 3.0* increases the number of cyber incidents or the number of customers affected by them, some customers may make the rational choice not to spend time and money seeking redress. The boundary problem (see Section 2.2.3) adds another layer of complexity with which many customers may be unprepared to deal effectively: overlapping legal frameworks mean that the same customers may have to use *different* dispute resolution mechanisms, depending on who receives the *same* data. As an example, in Australia, the statutory right of action available to customers as part of the Consumer Data Right does not apply to loss or damage caused by acts and omissions of trusted advisers. We argue that the mechanism for enforcing customer rights in a *CDS 3.0* framework should accommodate the underlying power imbalances and disincentivise the most vulnerable customers – individual consumers – from accepting uncompensated loss of their data and related risks as the more efficient option.

Second, the non-rivalrous[21] nature of customer data limits the range of acceptable remedies for affected customers. After all, unlike recovery of stolen money, recovery of stolen customer data is largely meaningless: at the current level of technology, stolen data can be copied infinitely, shared with an unlimited number of persons and even stored in distributed databases, which are very resilient to modification and destruction.[22]

Third, availability of customer redress may be limited by other factors – such as safe harbours which were discussed in greater detail in Section 5.2.3. In Australia, customers cannot use their statutory right of action for as long as the relevant service provider is able to rely on safe harbour protections, which grant *immunity* to any proceedings (whether civil or criminal). Despite any damage caused to the customer, the latter must bear the loss.

It follows, we argue, that the most vulnerable groups of customers in *CDS 3.0* frameworks, such as individual consumers, need to be supported by a redress mechanism that is both accessible and cheap. We propose a compensation mechanism with the following four key features.

First, it should eliminate the upfront costs of seeking compensation (just as bank customers do not have to individually sue their bank to recover their deposits under a deposit insurance scheme). Any obstacles to quick recovery by individual consumers need to be minimised, as the impact on such consumers is often immediate and quick action can help mitigate further damage. As an example, in the event of data loss enabling identity theft, individual consumers may need to replace their identity documents urgently. There appears to be no good policy reason to force individual consumers to bear the costs of such replacement and then bear even greater costs to bring an action against the service provider to obtain compensation. If nothing else, enabling individual consumers to act quickly can minimise the amount of compensation later.

Second, availability of customer compensation should not be prejudiced by the regulators' inaction – such as where the competent authority decides not to penalise the offender for whatever reason (such as a safe harbour defence).

Third, safe harbours should protect service providers against regulatory penalties but should have no impact on customer compensation. This limitation should help address the situation in Australia's CDR framework, where customers bear the residual risks of their service providers.[23] In the context of customer compensation, the end result of a service provider's actions (i.e., damage or loss to customers) should not be diminished by its good faith efforts to comply with the law. This is a deeply unsatisfactory outcome in a relationship between a professional and an unsophisticated customer. A close analogy would be the allocation of liability between banks and customers for payments made under a forged cheque under English and Australian case law.[24] Just as service providers in *CDS 3.0* frameworks have sought protection in the form of safe harbours, so did banks at the turn of the century seek to extend the customer's liability (and accordingly reduce their own).[25] The courts refused to grant banks the requested added protections against their customers and recognised that out of the two groups the more sophisticated party should absorb the loss:

> If they pay out upon cheques which are not his [customer's], they are acting outside their mandate and cannot plead his authority in justification of their debit to his account. This is a *risk of the service which it is their business to offer.*[26]

A similar logic should apply to service providers in a *CDS 3.0* framework, with similarly limited opportunities to avoid paying customer compensation. To continue the above analogy, an exception can be made where the customer contributed to the breach of its data (by analogy with bank customers who may prevent fraud by adopting simple precautions when executing cheques).[27] There is, however, no compelling reason to shield service providers from the consequences of their own actions – particularly in *CDS 3.0* frameworks where the customer does not control the computer systems used to store or share the data and thus should not be responsible for the safety of data held and transmitted.

Fourth, the amount of compensation should not be trivial and should prevent service providers from treating it as normal cost of doing business.

Compensation should reflect the opportunity for stolen data to be copied indefinitely and used repeatedly by different criminals, as well as the challenges in calculating the exact economic impact of each loss of customer data. Our proposed approach has two key advantages. It reflects the complex dynamics of the 'assume breach' approach to information security by emphasising customer recovery instead of incident prevention. In addition, it recognises that customer protections in *CDS 3.0* frameworks are likely to be supported by other mechanisms, such as mandatory professional insurance for service providers in Australia's Consumer Data Right framework. These mechanisms should not be based or priced on the assumption that many customers will choose not to enforce their rights as the more efficient course of action – instead, they need to ensure that *all* affected customers will be compensated *in full*. The limitations of one such mechanism, mandatory insurance, are discussed in the next section.

6.2   Limitations of insurance

Australia's Consumer Data Right framework demonstrates how mandatory insurance may be used as a regulatory tool to improve recoverability of sums due to customers. In particular, the *CDR Rules* require accredited persons to 'have adequate insurance, or a comparable guarantee, in light of the risk of CDR consumers not being properly compensated for any loss that might reasonably be expected to arise from a breach of obligations' under the CDR.[28] The list of eligible insurance products is not exhaustive, but the accreditation guidelines expressly mention two forms of insurance that may satisfy the obligation: 'professional indemnity insurance' and 'cyber insurance.'[29]

Mandatory insurance offers additional certainty that customer claims for compensation will be met by service providers. However, it has limitations that need to be acknowledged.

The first is determined by the legal nature of insurance. The CDR's insurance guidelines specify that '[t]he insurance policies must specify the accredited person as a named insured'[30] but are silent regarding the beneficiary. It follows that eligible insurance is likely to protect the accredited *service providers themselves* by letting them claim under the policy to satisfy customer claims, limiting the customers' ability to make a claim against the insurer.[31] This outcome is noticeably different from bank deposit insurance, which seeks to protect accountholders directly. In other words, insurance may help minimise the risk of insolvency of the accredited service provider but is much more limited in the event of insolvency. Interestingly, the most recent edition of the CDR insurance guidelines seems to acknowledge that 'insurance may give third-party claimants (including CDR consumers) greater protection than might otherwise be available as unsecured creditors in the insolvency'[32] but does not prescribe specific requirements that would ensure customers can claim as beneficiaries.

Second, recovery may be limited by the insurance policy exclusions and caps.[33] To tackle this issue, Australia's CDR insurance guidelines specify that the insurance parameters should be 'adequate' and list a range of factors that accredited persons need to consider – including two exclusions that must not be included in the insurance policy (in particular, exclusions regarding claims brought in the Australian Financial Complaints Authority and exclusions of liability for privacy and data related claims brought by customers).[34] Overall, however, the CDR's insurance guidelines offer substantial flexibility to accredited service providers:

> The CDR Rules do not contain strict prescriptive requirements for insurance because those requirements may not be appropriate in all cases. A prescriptive approach might cause accredited persons to be either underinsured or over-insured, or it may diminish their flexibility to obtain insurance that is appropriate for their business.[35]

We expect that some jurisdictions, particularly those with a less sophisticated insurance market, may instead choose to adopt a stricter approach and offer less flexibility, such as by providing a closed list of permitted exclusions.

Lastly, as long as the accredited person is the named insured, its own actions may negatively affect the amount payable by the insurer. Since customers (particularly individual consumers) may have limited capacity to monitor the insurance coverage of their service providers, we argue regulatory oversight is necessary and, depending on the situation, may require prompt adjustments to deal with any changes of the service provider's risk profile. The importance of an agile regulatory framework for *CDS 3.0* is discussed further in Section 7.2.

Notes

1 See Section 5.2.3.
2 Anton Didenko, 'Cybersecurity Regulation in the Financial Sector: Prospects of Legal Harmonization in the European Union and Beyond' (2020) 25(1) *Uniform Law Review* 128.
3 Reserve Bank of Australia, *Financial Stability Review* (Report, October 2021) 38 (emphasis added).
4 'Optus Data Breach', *Australian Government Department of Home Affairs Cyber and Infrastructure Security Centre* (Web Page, 30 September 2022) <www.cisc.gov.au/news-media/archive/article?itemId=945>.
5 'Medibank Private Limited and AHM Cyber Incident', *Australian Government Department of Home Affairs* (Web Page, 21 October 2022) <www.homeaffairs.gov.au/news-media/archive/article?itemId=961>.
6 'OAIC Statement on MyDeal Data Breach', *Office of the Australian Information Commissioner* (Web Page, 21 October 2022) <www.oaic.gov.au/updates/news-and-media/oaic-statement-on-mydeal-data-breach>.
7 See *Privacy Legislation Amendment (Enforcement and Other Measures) Act 2022* (Cth).

8 Australian Government, 'Federal Budget' (26 May 2023) *Consumer Data Right Newsletter.*
9 Australian Privacy Foundation, Submission to Treasury, *Inquiry into Future Directions for the Consumer Data Right* (Issues Paper, 6 May 2020) 2 <https://treasury. gov.au/sites/default/files/2020-07/australian-privacy-foundation.pdf>.
10 An alternative pathway exists for contraventions of certain credit reporting provisions, which enable individuals to apply for a compensation order, but this also involves several stages (proceedings can only be commenced against an entity once there is a civil penalty order against that entity or it has been found guilty of an offence): see *Privacy Act 1988* (Cth) ss 25, 25A.
11 As defined in the *Australian Information Commissioner Act 2010* (Cth).
12 *Privacy Act 1988* (Cth) s 36.
13 Ibid s 52(1).
14 Ibid s 55A.
15 Ibid s 6(1).
16 *Competition and Consumer Act 2010* (Cth) ss 56EY, 82(1)(d).
17 Attorney-General's Department, Australian Government, *Privacy Act Review* (Report, 2023) 15 <www.ag.gov.au/sites/default/files/2023-02/privacy-act-review-report_0.pdf>.
18 Ibid 279.
19 Katharine Kemp and David Vaile, Submission to Treasury, *Review into Open Banking in Australia* (Final Report, 23 March 2018) 9–10 [29].
20 See Section 2.1.
21 See Section 1.1.
22 See, e.g., Ross Buckley, Anton Didenko and Mia Trzecinski, 'Blockchain and Its Applications: A Conceptual Legal Primer' (2023) 26(2) *Journal of International Economic Law* 363.
23 See Section 5.2.3.
24 *London Joint Stock Bank Ltd v Macmillan and Arthur* [1918] AC 777; *Greenwood v Martins Bank Ltd* [1933] 1 KB 371.
25 *Tai Hing Cotton Mill Ltd v Liu Chong Hing Bank Ltd* [1986] AC 80.
26 Ibid 106.
27 The ePayments Code developed by ASIC could be a helpful starting point for determining whether a customer has contributed to the breach in a digital ecosystem: see ASIC, 'ePayments Code' (2 June 2022).
28 *Competition and Consumer (Consumer Data Right) Rules 2020* (Cth) r 5.12(2)(b).
29 Australian Government, 'Supplementary Accreditation Guidelines – Insurance (Version 2)' (Guidelines, December 2022) 6 ('Supplementary Accreditation Guidelines').
30 Ibid 8.
31 ASIC, *Compensation and Insurance Arrangements for AFS Licensees* (Regulatory Guide 126, July 2022) [RG126.23].
32 Supplementary Accreditation Guidelines (n 29) 2.
33 Richard St John, *Compensation Arrangements for Consumers of Financial Services* (Report, April 2012).
34 Supplementary Accreditation Guidelines (n 29) 8.
35 Ibid 4.

Chapter 7

Regulation: oversight and flexibility

Abstract

This chapter focuses on the key features of regulatory design in a *CDS 3.0* framework. *Sections 7.1.1* and *7.1.2* tackle the crucial challenge of selecting the appropriate regulatory structure to conduct the strategic development, review and oversight of a *CDS 3.0* regime. The functional reorganisation of the Consumer Data Right regulatory framework that occurred in Australia soon after the roll-out of open banking is used as an illustration of the underlying difficulties, which are then evaluated in the context of a broader, economy-wide *CDS* setting. Specifically, *Section 7.1.2* argues that a policy agency, not a regulator, should be in charge of devising the rules for a *CDS 3.0* ecosystem because this task requires a comprehensive grasp of the national economy, its complex nature and the envisioned path for its development. *Section 7.1.3* shows that to realise the objectives of *CDS 3.0* frameworks it is critical to ensure that these frameworks remain flexible and adaptable over time, and policymakers and regulators are prepared to acknowledge their mistakes and make amendments. *Section 7.2* then emphasises the importance of identifying appropriate performance metrics and criteria for the evaluation of success of *CDS 3.0* regimes (or lack thereof).

7.1 Designing a *CDS 3.0* framework

Compared to sectoral initiatives like open banking, designing a regulatory framework for *CDS 3.0* is a much more daunting task.

7.1.1 Selecting the regulatory structure

In particular, existing sectoral regulatory structures may be insufficiently flexible to accommodate an economy-wide data sharing regime. Indeed, given the wide sectoral diversity – banking, energy, telecommunications, transport, agriculture, health and medical services, insurance, retail and groceries, education and many more – it is hard to imagine how positioning the underlying regulatory infrastructure in any of the listed sectors could subsequently be meaningfully expanded to other economy sectors. The Review into Open Banking in Australia, for example, concluded that in light of the government's

DOI: 10.4324/9781003414216-7

intention to build an economy-wide data sharing ecosystem, implementing open banking through banking sector specific instruments in the *Corporations Act 2001* (Cth), or the *Australian Securities and Investments Commission Act 2001* (Cth) or by modifying current licensing requirements, would be suboptimal.[1]

Selecting a suitable legislative and regulatory structure that enables strategic development, review and oversight of an economy-wide *CDS 3.0* regime is of the utmost importance. While errors may be unavoidable, approaching this task with due care and attention is imperative, to ensure reasonable use of time, human resources and capital.

An entirely new – sector-agnostic – legislative framework could serve as an option for the establishment of third-generation *CDS* regimes. Indeed, at the inception phase of the CDR, the Australian Government's Productivity Commission recommended that a new Data Sharing and Release Act be created to regulate nation-wide data sharing.[2] The subsequent Review into Open Banking concluded, however, that the creation of such an act would be a major and tedious project that, if rushed, may likely lead to errors and unintended consequences.[3] Emphasising the significance of simplicity and straightforward implementation, the review opted for the design that minimised the need for duplication of already existing legislation and meaningfully built upon existing legislative and regulatory arrangements, above all the *CCA* and the *Privacy Act 1988* (Cth) (see also Section 2.2.1).

It noted, however, that recourse to legislation – which is typically time-consuming and difficult to amend – should be reserved for 'those ideas and principles that are intended to last' and to fill any regulatory gaps, such as establishing ministerial authority to apply the CDR to new economy sectors and data sets and establish the parameters for subsidiary rule-making.[4] These subsidiary instruments (including regulations, ministerial determinations, etc.) would give effect to the legislative principles and provisions when the fast pace of technological change requires a quicker but also more detailed response to a problem. These instruments would also be well positioned to set expectations of what the *CDS 3.0* regime will deliver for each sector and determine the criteria as to how those expectations should be met.[5] Finally, considering that the regulatory framework would apply to technology, standards would play a crucial role in operationalising the legislation and rules by establishing a foundational level for the technical aspects of the relevant sector's customer data sharing system.

As a result, the CDR is embedded in the *CCA* (Part IVD) – an obvious choice given that it governs decision-making in a customer and competition-focused environment. This primary legislation is given effect through subsidiary instruments, namely sector designation instruments, *CDR Rules* and technical data standards as illustrated in Sections 1.5 and 3.1. Notably, New Zealand's draft legislation strongly resembles the Australian approach in that it proposes an 'umbrella' framework for a consumer data right in New Zealand with more detailed regulations (including 'designation regulations' and 'other regulations') and standards supporting the primary legislation.[6]

7.1.2 Rule-setting and compliance authorities

Identifying authorities most suitably positioned to oversee the development and implementation of *CDS 3.0* systems is a task of no less importance. Potential options include a *'co-regulatory' model* with multiple regulators involved in the design and enforcement of relevant rules or a *'division of responsibilities' model*, with the rule-setting authority resting with a policy agency and the enforcement powers lying with relevant regulators.

Drawing from the example of the UK open banking model with multiple regulators – where an order requiring to implement open banking was issued by the Competition and Markets Authority (CMA), while the Financial Conduct Authority (FCA) is responsible for the authorisation, supervision and regulation of open banking participants and the Information Commissioner's Office is in charge of data and privacy protection – Australia identified two existing key regulators, namely the ACCC and the OAIC, and established the DSB.[7] The ACCC – an independent government body in charge of enforcing competition and consumer protection laws – was tasked with evaluating economy sectors suitable for inclusion in the CDR and crafting sector-specific regulations.[8] The OAIC – responsible for overseeing privacy and information management practices in Australia – was entrusted with overseeing privacy and confidentiality matters.[9] The task of establishing standards concerning the format and procedures for data provision to customers and ADRs was given to the Data Standards Chair to be assisted by the DSB (initially, Data61 of the Commonwealth Scientific and Industrial Research Organisation (CSIRO).[10] The Treasury was given the authority to apply the CDR to new economy sectors. The decision to accord the rule-making powers to the ACCC was defended on the grounds that it would optimise flexibility and facilitate more extensive consultation with the CDR participants. Simultaneously, mandating Ministerial approval for the *CDR Rules* would establish a mechanism for checks and balances, ensuring that the rules are in harmony with the policies of the Australian government.[11]

However, shortly after the introduction of open banking, Australia had to admit its miscalculation. Concerns had been raised on numerous occasions regarding the needless fragmentation of the CDR framework, with responsibilities shared by the Treasury, ACCC, OAIC and Data61.[12] In response, a legislative amendment transferred the duty of sectoral examination and rule development from the regulator, ACCC, to the policy agency, the Treasury.[13] As a result, the Secretary of Treasury who heads the government department must conduct consultations with relevant stakeholders on the sectors to be designated under the CDR and provide a report to the Minister, who has the authority to designate the sector. The Treasury has also taken on the rule-making responsibility with the requirement to consult with the ACCC, OAIC or an entity identified by the Secretary of the Treasury as the primary sector regulator, and potentially other stakeholders as may be required by legislation.[14] This reorganisation is regarded as allowing for a more efficient and cohesive strategy for crafting and executing CDR policies, rules, and standards.[15]

By way of trial and error, Australian authorities concluded that the advancement of comprehensive data sharing processes across the economy should be spearheaded by a policy agency rather than a regulator.

Notably, recent developments in the UK and New Zealand suggest that both jurisdictions, in principle, appear to follow in the footsteps of Australia albeit adding some features reflective of certain national preferences.

Specifically, the 2020 *UK National Data Strategy*[16] emphasised Smart Data as a vital initiative aligning with the government's mission to maximise the value of data beyond banking. This initiative reflects the objectives of *CDS 3.0*, focusing on a cross-sectoral secure sharing of data.[17] Initially, the UK regulators were anticipated to play a central role in Smart Data's development, guiding activities, setting standards and encouraging industry and consumer involvement in data sharing.[18] Later, however, as consultations on data sharing in various UK sectors were occurring simultaneously, the Department for Business, Energy and Industrial Strategy (BEIS) took charge of coordinating Smart Data policy.[19] In April 2023, the BEIS established a Smart Data Council tasked with establishing, guiding and coordinating novel schemes that harness the potential of Smart Data. The Council comprises key government departments, regulatory authorities, industry bodies and consumer representative groups, such as HM Treasury, the CMA, the Information Commissioner's Office, representatives from Citizen's Advice, the Coalition for a Digital Economy (COADEC) and other stakeholders.[20] In contrast to the Australian approach, where the Treasury must consult on the sector-designation and rule-making with relevant regulators (the ACCC, the OAIC and such other primary sector regulators as may be needed) as well as other stakeholders, the UK has opted for a 'standing' consultative mechanism comprising the relevant expertise.

Further, like Australia, the UK currently proposes a scheme where relevant departments responsible for developing policy objectives and monitoring their progress are invested with the powers to regulate economy-wide customer data sharing to deliver on the UK's National Data Strategy objectives – *the Data Protection and Digital Information No. 2 (DPDI) Bill* was laid before Parliament in March 2023.[21] The bill proposes enabling legislation for Smart Data and confers powers on the secretaries of state and the Treasury to establish and mandate participation in Smart Data schemes via secondary legislation in the form of regulations,[22] specifically, on matters 'in connection with access to customer data and business data' (including regulations requiring data holders to provide customer data),[23] procedures 'by which customers authorise persons to receive, or act on their behalf in relation to, customer data,'[24] and regulations on monitoring compliance and ensuring enforcement.[25]

A similar strategy has been adopted in New Zealand, where the proposed *Customer and Product Data Act 2023* envisages that the Governor General – His Majesty The King's representative in New Zealand – as advised by the Executive Council comprising all Ministers of the Crown, may issue such regulations as may be required under the Act. Regulations addressing sector designation (i.e., those that designate the data holders and classes of data[26]), are proposed to be made on the recommendations by the Minister responsible for the administration of the Act.[27]

The paths taken in Australia, the UK and New Zealand strongly suggest the design of a fundamentally new system – such as *CDS 3.0* – is not just a regulatory issue. The process entails a comprehensive grasp of the national economy, its complex mosaic nature and the intended path for its advancement. It must be based on an understanding and acknowledgment of the distinct strengths, needs and difficulties that various sectors of the economy might be confronting. It calls for a readiness to think laterally and, where necessary, take risks. Leading this process demands the capability and expertise to analyse policy matters from a holistic economic standpoint, going well beyond a mere regulatory focus.[28]

We do not suggest, however, that the current CDR governance framework is set in stone. As mentioned in Section 4.1, the submissions to the Statutory Review of the CDR highlighted that – despite significant developments of the framework since its establishment in 2019 – the challenges of implementing the CDR and engaging with its administrators have been compounded by the complexity inherent in dealing with multiple regulators, alleged poor coordination between the regulators and a perceived lack of tools to support CDR participants.[29]

Many participants therefore explicitly advocated for the creation of a specialist entity tasked with the implementation of the CDR, such as the Open Banking Implementation Entity (OBIE) in the UK.[30] They reasoned that such an entity would not only function as reservoir of extensive technical knowledge in the field of data and requisite IT support infrastructure but also maintain a single voice and deliver necessary education, particularly relevant for smaller participants currently struggling to access the CDR and lacking the necessary financial resources and technical expertise to participate in the system.[31] The ACCC – the very agency tasked with the accreditation and enforcement of the CDR – admitted that it 'is supportive of a specialist agency being tasked with the implementation of the CDR'; and welcomes 'a functional separation of the entities responsible for the rule-making, operations and enforcement.'[32] Likewise, some other participants opined that the accreditation and enforcement functions currently consolidated under the ACCC could be divorced from each other. They pointed to the strong perception among industry members that responsibility for onboarding new participants inhibits effective enforcement of the CDR.[33]

The Review pushed back on both propositions, however. It reasoned that the concept of an OBIE-like entity – time limited to the implementation of sharing certain type of data (i.e., payment account data) and funded through industry (i.e., the nine largest banks in the UK that have been mandated to open up customer data) – was not readily transferrable to facilitating the policy objectives of an economy-wide initiative like the CDR. It also stressed that adding another entity could result in the fragmentation of the CDR. Crucially, since none of the submissions suggested how such an entity should be financed, and funding by the government would divert limited resources from other important initiatives, the Review concluded that no space for an OBIE-like entity was available under the current CDR framework.[34] The Review also noted that separating accreditation and operational responsibilities from the agency charged with enforcing the CDR risks leading to conflicting interpretations of the *CDR Rules*; for the lack of a better alternative, it concluded that the accreditation, monitoring and enforcement responsibilities should stay with the ACCC for now.[35] That said, the Review also recommended that as the CDR matures, implementation and regulatory measures should be revised in the future.[36]

7.1.3 'Living frameworks'

Irrespective of the sectors involved in domestic data sharing frameworks, *CDS 3.0* regimes must remain dynamic, that is, 'living,' being open to acknowledging their shortcomings and adapting accordingly.[37] This adaptability is essential because changes in customer and business preferences, as well as technological innovation, tend to unfold more rapidly than the evolution of regulatory frameworks.

Moreover, regulation of third-generation *CDS* systems involves an ongoing process of 'learning by doing.' These systems are inherently complex and will need to be responsive to the requirements and capacity of the domestic economy. They will necessarily involve a multitude of stakeholders – policy agencies, regulators, standard setting authorities, data holders, data recipients, technology solution providers and customers – each contributing to the development and implementation of the regime in their own way. Assessing the full scope, impact and dynamics of the interactions between these stakeholders is plainly impossible at the design and drafting phase of the regime. Rather, *CDS 3.0* systems are likely to be continuously informed by the experiences and insights drawn from their earlier stages of development. Notably, because of diverse jurisdictional demands, even as *CDS 3.0* frameworks emerge and mature elsewhere precedents to draw inspiration and learnings from may remain limited requiring domestic authorities to show foresight and ingenuity while carefully balancing the risks and advantages of such systems. Since CDR's launch in July 2020, it continues to evolve, receiving consistent constructive feedback from its stakeholders. Several policy and regulatory determinations, as illustrated earlier, were substantial. This included the shifting of rule-making powers from the ACCC to the Federal Treasury, the introduction of new tiers of accreditation and the exemption of trusted advisers from the accreditation requirements (see Sections 4.1 and 4.2).

7.2   Performance metrics

For effective and efficient *CDS 3.0* frameworks, we propose the establishment of performance metrics. Such metrics help assess the impact of third-generation *CDS* regimes by providing an objective basis for evaluating whether the regime's outcomes are aligned with its objectives. Performance metrics also clarify expectations of regime participants and serve to deter potential abuses of the *CDS* regime. Given third-generation *CDS* frameworks are likely to develop sector-by-sector rather than be launched across many sectors at once (see Section 3.1), performance metrics in one sector may guide what may or may not be achievable in other sectors.[38] Importantly, publicly available performance metrics foster transparency and comprehensibility of the regime's benefits and the challenges it may be facing, leading to more informed and responsible customer engagement with the system.[39]

In Australia, evaluation and assessment of the CDR's operation have been recommended at different stages of its development and implementation,[40] yet no formal or structured list of criteria for measuring its success *across all of the CDR's key objectives* has been promulgated (see also Section 1.6). Currently, the CDR website offers some information on providers accredited to offer services under the CDR[41] and on the system's functioning in banking, including on active data holders' performance and average service availability.[42] However, as rightly observed by the Statutory Review of the CDR, this data offers merely 'a starting point for participants and the public' and should be complemented by further data points relevant to the use and growth of the system.[43] In contrast, under the UK's open banking framework, impact reports have been published since early 2021 to measure the ecosystem's growth and value for its users.[44] While focused on banking, these reports are comprehensive and include a detailed analysis of the ongoing expansion and uptake of UK open banking and customer experiences with open banking-enabled services as determined by customer surveys. While we do not suggest these impact reports should be slavishly emulated for the CDR or any other *CDS 3.0* framework, they undoubtedly provide valuable insights for shaping the metrics for customer data sharing systems and the methodology for tracking progress against these metrics.

Certainly, creating performance criteria for complex systems like *CDS 3.0* – that involve many different stakeholders with potentially conflicting interests and require sensitivity to sector-specific nuances – is challenging. Importantly, to facilitate a comprehensive assessment of the regime's effectiveness on a macro level and in individual economy sectors, metrics must align with the regime's objectives (see Section 1.6). Crucially, for systems that strive to achieve multiple – at times competing – purposes, as *CDS 3.0* do,[45] it is important to ensure some goals are not achieved at the expense of others. Performance metrics will therefore need to reflect the delicate balance that needs to be struck among multiple objectives of *CDS 3.0* frameworks. In particular, when devising criteria to assess whether increased competition has been promoted (such as numbers of new players entering the customer data sharing system in a given sector and indicators of decreasing information asymmetry), it is important to do so with a view to the customer protection objective. Criteria to show compliance with the latter could be comparable to those used to measure improved competition. For example, improved customer protection could be measured by the volume of data breaches within the regime relative to those in the broader economy, reduced reliance on less secure methods of data sharing, such as SS, and other indicators.[46] Furthermore, if *CDS 3.0* regimes are expected to be ever-evolving frameworks (as discussed in Section 7.1.3), it follows that performance metrics are likely to require revision and adjustments over time. For instance, over time, jurisdictions considering joining a cross-border *CDS* may need to align their performance metrics with relevant international data sharing standards and practices (see Section 3.3).

In the Australian context, we therefore welcome recommendation 1.5 of the Statutory Review which provides that measures to assess the overall performance of the CDR, including its ability to deliver meaningful outcomes for customers, be devised and made public to 'provide increased confidence and assurance to participants.'[47] Considering the enthusiasm of industry and customer representative groups to collaborate with relevant authorities in defining these metrics (as evidenced by submissions to the Statutory Review and the strategic assessment consultation[48]), it is highly probable that the challenges associated with this endeavour will be collectively addressed and resolved. As the next step, regular reports from the ACCC or Treasury on such metrics and the extent to which they are met should serve a salutary function in raising awareness of and fostering confidence in the CDR system and may one day inform the design of performance metrics in other *CDS 3.0* regimes.

Notes

1 Treasury, Australian Government, *Review into Open Banking: Giving Customers Choice, Convenience and Confidence* (Report, December 2017) 13 ('*Review into Open Banking*').

2 Productivity Commission, Australian Government, *Data Availability and Use* (Inquiry Report No 82, 31 March 2017) 2.
3 *Review into Open Banking* (n 1) 11.
4 Ibid.
5 Ibid 11–2.
6 See Customer and Product Data Bill (Draft for Consultation) (NZ) ss 3(1), 4(4), 27–9 <www.mbie.govt.nz/assets/exposure-draft-customer-and-product-data-bill.pdf> ('Customer and Product Data Bill').
7 Treasury, Australian Government, 'Consumer Data Right Overview' (Booklet, September 2019) 9.
8 Ibid 10.
9 Ibid.
10 Explanatory Memorandum, Treasury Laws Amendment (Consumer Data Right) Bill 2019 (Cth) [1.15]. Note that the Data Standards Body has later been placed within Treasury: see 'Introduction.' *Consumer Data Standards* (Web Page) <https://consumerdatastandardsaustralia.github.io/standards/#introduction>.
11 *Review into Open Banking* (n 1) 18.
12 See, e.g., Denham Sadler, 'Consumer Data Right Powers Shifted from ACCC', *InnovationAus.com* (Online, 6 November 2020) <www.innovationaus.com/consumer-data-right-powers-shifted-from-accc/>; 'Frydenberg Takes Back Some Ground from the Regulators', *BankingDay* (Online, 3 December 2020) <www.bankingday.com/login?p=%2ffrydenberg-takes-back-ground-from-regulators>.
13 See *Treasury Laws Amendment (2020 Measures No 6) Act 2020* (Cth) sch 2.
14 See ibid cls 31, 34.
15 See Paul Franklin, 'Important Changes for the Consumer Data Right Program' (3 March 2021) *Consumer Data Right Newsletter*.
16 Department for Digital, Culture, Media & Sport, UK Government, 'National Data Strategy' (Policy Paper, 9 December 2020) <www.gov.uk/government/publications/uk-national-data-strategy/national-data-strategy>.
17 Ibid.
18 Department for Business, Energy and Industrial Strategy (UK), 'Modernising Consumer Markets' (Consumer Green Paper, April 2018) 23 [63].
19 With FCA leading the development of data-sharing arrangements in banking and finance, Ofcom in communications, Ofgem in energy, and DWP (Department for Work and Pensions) in pensions: Department for Business, Energy and Industrial Strategy (UK), *Smart Data Working Group: Spring 2021 Report* (Report, June 2021) 7.
20 Department for Business and Trade and Kevin Hollinrake MP, 'New Smart Data Council to Drive Forward Savings for Household Bills' (Press Release, 17 April 2023) <www.gov.uk/government/news/new-smart-data-council-to-drive-forward-savings-for-household-bills>.
21 For more details, see 'Data Protection and Digital Information Bill', *UK Parliament* (Web Page, 5 May 2023) <https://bills.parliament.uk/bills/3322>. See also 'Smart Data: The UK's New Data Sharing Laws Will Spur Innovation and Improve Consumer Outcomes', *TechUK* (Online, 15 March 2023) <www.techuk.org/resource/smart-data-the-uk-s-new-data-sharing-laws-will-spur-innovation-and-improve-consumer-outcomes.html>.
22 Joint Regulatory Oversight Committee, 'Recommendations for the Next Phase of Open Banking in the UK' (Policy Paper, 17 April 2023) [1.5].
23 Data Protection and Digital Information Bill (UK) pt 3 ss 61(1), 62(1).
24 Ibid pt 3 s 63(3).
25 Ibid pt 3 ss 66–7.

26 See Customer and Product Data Bill (n 6) 4(4).

27 See ibid ss 5, 59.

28 See Ross Buckley, Natalia Jevglevskaja and Scott Farrell, 'Australia's Data Sharing Regime: Six Lessons for Europe' (2022) 33(1) *King's Law Journal* 61, 82.

29 Treasury, Australian Government, *Statutory Review of the Consumer Data Right* (Report, 2022) 35 ('*Statutory Review*').

30 See, for example, TrueLayer, 'TrueLayer Response to Statutory Review of the Consumer Data Right' (Submission, 20 May 2022) 12–3 <https://treasury.gov.au/sites/default/files/2022-09/c2022-314513-truelayer.pdf>; ABA, Submission to Treasury, *Statutory Review of the Consumer Data Right* (20 May 2022) 5 <https://treasury.gov.au/sites/default/files/2022-09/c2022-314513-australian_banking_association.pdf>.

31 See also *Statutory Review* (n 29) 36.

32 See ACCC, Submission to Treasury, *Statutory Review of the Consumer Data Right* (May 2022) 7 <https://treasury.gov.au/sites/default/files/2022-09/c2022-314513-australian_competition_and_consumer_commission.pdf>.

33 *Statutory Review* (n 29) 32.

34 Ibid 36.

35 Ibid 32.

36 Ibid 37, recommendation 2.3.

37 Buckley, Jevglevskaja and Farrell (n 28) 83.

38 Telstra, Submission to Treasury, *Statutory Review of the Consumer Data Right* (20 May 2022), 2–3 <https://treasury.gov.au/sites/default/files/2022-09/c2022-314513-telstra.pdf>.

39 *Statutory Review* (n 29) 28; FinTech Australia, Submission to Treasury, *Statutory Review of the Consumer Data Right* (May 2022) 10 <https://treasury.gov.au/sites/default/files/2022-09/c2022-314513-fintech_australia.pdf>.

40 *Review into Open Banking* (n 1) recommendation 6.6; Treasury, Australian Government, *Inquiry into Future Directions for the Consumer Data Right* (Report, October 2020) recommendation 7.7. Statutory review of Part IVD ('Consumer Data Right') was required under *Competition and Consumer Act 2010* (Cth) s 56GH.

41 See 'Current Providers', *Consumer Data Right* (Web Page) <www.cdr.gov.au/find-a-provider>.

42 See 'Performance', *Consumer Data Right* (Web Page) <www.cdr.gov.au/performance>.

43 *Statutory Review* (n 29) 28.

44 See Open Banking UK, *The Open Banking Impact Report* (Report, June 2022); Open Banking, *The Open Banking Impact Report* (Report, October 2021).

45 See discussion in Section 2.2.2.

46 See also Sections 4.2 and 5.2.

47 *Statutory Review* (n 29) 29.

48 See 'Consumer Data Right: Strategic Assessment', *Treasury.gov.au* (Web Page) <https://treasury.gov.au/consultation/c2021-198050>; Treasury, Australian Government, *Strategic Assessment: Outcomes* (Report, January 2022). For stakeholder engagement, see, e.g., Consumer Policy Research Centre, Submission to Treasury, *Consumer Data Right – Strategic Assessment* (26 August 2021) 2–3 <https://cprc.org.au/wp-content/uploads/2021/11/CPRC-Submission-Consumer-Data-Right-Strategic-Assessment-August-2021.pdf>.

Chapter 8

Conclusions: twelve lessons for the world

Abstract

This chapter summarises our conclusions from previous chapters and formulates the key lessons for the design of *CDS 3.0* frameworks. While these are largely informed by our analysis of Australia's Consumer Data Right, it is hoped many of the lessons will be relevant for other third-generation *CDS* ecosystems.

8.1 A better taxonomy is needed for customer data sharing frameworks

Existing terminology for the different models for the sharing of valuable customer data is imprecise, often confusing and therefore unsatisfactory. This book offers a taxonomy which distinguishes three generations of customer data sharing frameworks. *CDS 1.0* regimes rely on pre-existing (e.g., privacy and competition) laws. *CDS 2.0* frameworks are purpose-built to facilitate *customer data sharing* but are limited to a single sector (e.g., finance). *CDS 3.0* frameworks apply on a cross-sectoral, possibly economy-wide, basis. While *CDS 2.0* and *CDS 3.0* share similar objectives and mechanics, the broader scope of *CDS 3.0* generates distinctive benefits, risks and regulatory challenges.

Australia's Consumer Data Right is the only fully operational *CDS 3.0* framework at the time of writing, and serves as a working example of a gradual, sector-by-sector progression towards an economy-wide customer data sharing regime. We anticipate most *CDS 3.0* frameworks will follow a similar journey.

8.2 *CDS 3.0* frameworks should recognise the distinctive needs of different customer types

In principle, *CDS 3.0* frameworks can be designed to accommodate all kinds of customers, including businesses and individuals. However, we argue that a

DOI: 10.4324/9781003414216-8

'one-size-fits-all' approach is not appropriate and suggest that *CDS 3.0* frameworks for more vulnerable customer types, particularly individual consumers, should incorporate additional protections. Examples include the proposed principle 'same data, same risks, same controls' (Section 5.2.2), a centralised hub for 'direct-to-customer' disclosures (see Section 5.2.4), additional measures to raise consumers' awareness of the risks of engaging with the *CDS* framework (Section 5.2.5), and ease of enforcement (Section 6.1).

Conversely, business customers may benefit from extra flexibility such as permission to choose the recipients of their data without restriction (see Section 4.2.5). We argue the lack of expertise of one group of customers, like individual consumers, should not limit the ability of other customer types (like corporations) to make use of their data – such as through 'direct-to-customer' disclosures (see Section 5.2.4).

8.3   Policymakers should address conflicts of CDS 3.0 frameworks with other laws

When designing new frameworks for the sharing of customer data, policymakers should identify other laws which may conflict with the *CDS 3.0* regime and establish clear boundaries between them. Our research shows that potentially conflicting provisions can be found in competition laws, consumer (protection) laws and laws dealing with privacy and information security (see Section 2.2). At the same time, *CDS 3.0* frameworks need not be self-contained: where the objectives of *CDS 3.0* and pre-existing laws are aligned, duplication is unnecessary.

With the gradual expansion of *CDS 3.0* frameworks to new sectors (as opposed to an instant economy-wide roll-out, which we do not expect to be common), *CDS 3.0* will initially apply as an exception from existing privacy and information security laws. However, as it covers most of the economy, becoming the dominant framework for customer data sharing, the exception will become the norm. We argue, therefore, that in the long-term overlapping 'general' legal frameworks will need to be adjusted to align with *CDS 3.0*. From this perspective, *CDS 3.0* frameworks can be used as 'testing laboratories' to prepare for the typically much-needed, economy-wide reforms of privacy and information security laws (see Section 2.2.3).

8.4   Action initiation should be integrated in CDS 3.0 frameworks

For *CDS 3.0* frameworks to fully unlock value for customers, they must facilitate action initiation. As demonstrated in Section 3.2, action initiation, developed to provide customers with the capability to authorise a service provider to undertake actions on their behalf, will turbo-charge *CDS 3.0* systems.

Compared to the functionality of mere data *sharing*, action initiation brings to the market a much broader range of products and services. Without action initiation, *CDS 3.0* systems remain rudimentary and offer customers little more than comparison platforms. Because of the seamless, potentially nearly instant, switching between products and services that action initiation makes possible, we argue this functionality promises to eliminate loyalty penalties and restore what we call 'a commercial morality,' a basic fairness, that modern businesses often neglect (see Section 3.2).

8.5 *CDS 3.0* frameworks should balance out accreditation requirements and data security

The effectiveness of *CDS 3.0* systems hinges on customers' confidence in the secure handling of their data by service providers within these systems. From a customer's perspective, accreditation displays the service providers' ability and commitment to adhere diligently to *CDS 3.0* safety and security standards and thus appropriately manage data that customers choose to share with them.

In designing accreditation regimes, however, policymakers should be mindful of not imposing overly burdensome expectations on service providers. While accreditation creates an equitable competitive environment for businesses and opens *CDS 3.0* ecosystems to successful candidates, excessively stringent accreditation criteria risk discouraging service providers from joining the regime, thus, ultimately, diminishing its benefits for customers. Policymakers therefore need to find the appropriate equilibrium between ensuring safe and secure flows of customer data and service providers' ability and interest in becoming part of a *CDS 3.0* regime.

8.6 Harmful data-sharing practices competing with *CDS 3.0* frameworks should be restricted or banned

While screen-scraping may offer service providers a range of benefits (see Section 4.3), our analysis in Section 5.2.2 shows that the associated risks to especially individual consumers can be severe. We argue, therefore, that the law should intervene to restrict or prohibit screen-scraping for several reasons. While we recognise that not all uses of screen-scraping will cause immediate harm to consumers, difficulties with distinguishing 'legal' screen-scraping from illegal automation forces service providers to adopt indiscriminate measures like whitelisting IP addresses of known data aggregators – which can be abused by attackers. Furthermore, if left unattended screen-scraping may create perverse incentives for service providers operating in a *CDS 3.0* ecosystem, who may simply opt to maintain *both* streams of customer data instead of choosing one over the other – disregarding the risks to customers.

8.7 Customer trust should be the key driver of *CDS 3.0* development and subsequent revisions

Without customer trust, a *CDS 3.0* framework may lack its object (customer data) and its purpose. After all, the decision to use *CDS 3.0* channels or alternative data sharing methods remains in the hands of the customer, as the *CDS 3.0* ecosystem is designed around voluntary interaction of customers with different service providers. Without customer trust, such interaction is impossible (see Section 5.1). Importantly, customer trust in a *CDS 3.0* framework is *institutional and impersonal*: customers do not need to trust each individual or business involved in the circulation of their data and can rely on the system as a whole.

Complex dynamics of multi-sectoral *CDS 3.0* frameworks suggest that the results of their implementation in one sector (whether positive or negative) may have spill-over effects on other sectors. On the one hand, successful implementation in finance could boost the level of trust customers place in the entire *CDS 3.0* ecosystem and positively affect its roll-out in energy or telecommunications. On the other hand, breaches of customer data in those sectors may impact the customers' perception of *CDS 3.0* in finance.

We identify five main enablers of customer trust in *CDS 3.0* frameworks: (i) accreditation, (ii) information security and privacy, (iii) customer redress, (iv) customer empowerment and (v) customer experience and awareness (see Section 5.2).

8.8 Enforcement of customer protections in *CDS 3.0* frameworks should balance fairness and efficiency

Our analysis in Section 6.1 suggests that ease of enforcement is a crucial component of *CDS 3.0* frameworks, particularly when other elements of those frameworks (such as accreditation or information security requirements) fail to prevent damage to the customer. The twin notions of fairness and efficiency underpin our conclusion. The 'assume breach' logic commonly used in the context of information security implies that every computer system will be breached at some point and thus the integrity of customer data cannot be guaranteed. It follows that depriving the customer of meaningful recourse *ex post* (i.e., after the breach) will be grossly *unfair*, since the customer bears the resulting risks, including identity theft. However, even if enforcement is theoretically possible in the context of *CDS 3.0* frameworks, it may be undermined by a range of factors, such as (i) lack of a direct claim against the service provider, (ii) unduly burdensome costs for less sophisticated customers and (iii) limitations of insurance as a tool to improve recoverability of sums due to customers.

Some regulatory tools, like safe harbours, may appear to be an attractive means of encouraging service providers to engage with *CDS 3.0* by shielding them from liability. However, the adoption of such tools needs to be approached with caution as they tend to reward service providers for *formal* compliance, while placing the cost of provider errors upon the parties least well placed to bear those costs – the customers. We argue this outcome is inappropriate for a customer-oriented *CDS 3.0* framework that relies on customer trust to function well.

8.9 In the long term, *CDS 3.0* systems should be mandated

While in the short to medium term, the objectives of *CDS 3.0* frameworks may be achieved without direct regulatory intervention, we argue in favour of mandating a customer data sharing regime in the long term. Mandatory regimes are much better positioned to address the risks of market concentration. In particular, as shown in Section 2.1, economies of scale and scope combined with network effects enable data aggregators to offer superior products and services at lower costs per user, effectively pushing competitors out of the market. Facilitative or market-driven approaches to *CDS* are unlikely to tackle the risk of monopolisation of different economy sectors by data aggregators with the same efficiency. Furthermore, mandated *CDS* regimes are well placed to explicitly address both potential deficits of pre-existing legal frameworks as well as possible overlaps with these frameworks (above all competition laws, consumer protection laws and laws dealing with privacy and information security, see Sections 2.2 and 8.3), thus facilitating effective implementation. Importantly, mandated *CDS 3.0* can also effectively eliminate alternative insecure customer data sharing practices such as screen scraping (see Section 5.2.2).

8.10 Economy-wide *CDS 3.0* frameworks should be driven by a policy agency, not a regulator

Identifying the authorities most suitably placed to oversee the design and implementation of *CDS 3.0* systems is vital. We argue that a policy agency rather than a regulator should lead the development of economy-wide data sharing processes, as creating a novel and multifaceted system – such as a *CDS 3.0* regime – requires a holistic understanding of a national economy, its inherent complexity and the envisioned path for its development. It also requires appreciation of the unique strengths, needs and challenges encountered by distinct sectors within the economy and a commitment not to exacerbate these challenges when individual sectors become part of standardised economy-wide data sharing processes. Guiding this complex process demands the capacity and expertise of a policy agency, not merely a regulatory outlook.

8.11 Legislative and regulatory structures matter in CDS 3.0 regimes

We argue that in jurisdictions that have chosen or are considering a prescriptive approach to *CDS* careful attention should be given to selecting a legislative and regulatory structure that enables strategic development, review and oversight of a given *CDS 3.0* regime. While errors may be unavoidable, approaching this task carefully is imperative, to ensure reasonable use of financial and human resources and realisation of the objectives of third-generation *CDS* regimes. While existing sectoral regulatory structures may be insufficiently flexible to accommodate cross-sectoral or economy-wide data sharing, alternative approaches may include devising a novel, sector-agnostic, *CDS 3.0* framework 'from scratch' or integrating *CDS* into existing legislative and regulatory amendments and building upon them over time. Each approach offers its distinct benefits, and its own challenges. Whichever approach is adopted, developing a *CDS 3.0* regime will be a learning-by-doing exercise in each individual jurisdiction. Australia's experience suggests such regimes need to be treated as living structures that need regular refinement and adjustment.

8.12 To improve efficiency of CDS 3.0 frameworks, performance metrics need to be established

To ensure *CDS 3.0* systems develop effectively and efficiently, it is imperative to establish performance metrics. Such metrics will help relevant authorities (policy agencies and regulators), industry, customer representative groups and the public to understand how well a *CDS 3.0* regime is performing and whether it is achieving its intended goals. However, devising appropriate metrics may be a daunting task: just as *CDS* frameworks must delicately balance their multiple objectives, so too must the performance metrics. Involvement of relevant stakeholders is therefore desirable to ensure these metrics reflect the abilities and interests of those who will be driving the third-generation *CDS*.

Index